SUFFOLK RECORDS SOCIETY

SUFFOLK CHARTERS

*Founding Editor*
*the late Professor R. Allen Brown*

XV

# CHARTERS OF
# ST BARTHOLOMEW'S PRIORY
# SUDBURY

The Benedictine priory of St Bartholomew, outside Sudbury, Suffolk, was a cell of Westminster Abbey founded in the reign of Henry I by Wulfric the moneyer. Although a small and poorly-endowed establishment, it has nevertheless, and unusually, left over 130 original documents in the muniments at Westminster, enabling this volume in the Suffolk Charters series to be the first to be devoted to a group of original documents rather than medieval transcriptions. Dating mostly from the thirteenth and early fourteenth centuries and including grants and land transactions between local townsmen and small landholders as well as donations to the priory, the collection illustrates the lower levels of local society and the government of the town, providing a wealth of evidence for trades and occupations, place names and personal names in the Sudbury area, including the earliest known reeves and mayors of Sudbury. Of particular interest are a late fourteenth-century inventory of the priory which brings alive the physical surroundings of the monks, and the quantities of seals attached to the charters, including an unusual number of women's seals. There are also a number of deeds relating to the family of Simon Thebaud, the Simon 'of Sudbury' who became archbishop of Canterbury in 1375.

RICHARD MORTIMER has been Keeper of Muniments, Westminster Abbey, since 1986; he has edited four previous volumes in the Suffolk Charters series.

SUFFOLK RECORDS SOCIETY

SUFFOLK CHARTERS

ISSN 0261-9938

*General Editor*
Professor Christopher Harper-Bill

*External Advisors*

Previously published volumes of Suffolk Charters
are listed at the back of this volume.

# CHARTERS OF
# ST BARTHOLOMEW'S PRIORY
# SUDBURY

**Edited by Richard Mortimer**

The Boydell Press

Suffolk Records Society

First published 1996


Published for the Suffolk Records Society
by The Boydell Press
an imprint of Boydell & Brewer Ltd
PO Box 9, Woodbridge, Suffolk IP12 3DF, UK
and of Boydell & Brewer Inc.
PO Box 41026, Rochester, NY 14604–4126, USA


ISBN 0 85115 574 X


British Library Cataloguing-in-Publication Data
Charters of St. Bartholomew's Priory, Sudbury. – (Suffolk
    Charters ; v. 15)
    1. St. Bartholomew's Priory – Charters 2. Suffolk
    (England) – Charters
    I. Mortimer, Richard    II. Suffolk Records Society
    333.3'22'094264
    ISBN 085115574X

This publication is printed on acid-free paper

Printed in Great Britain by
St Edmundsbury Press Ltd, Bury St Edmunds, Suffolk

# CONTENTS

# GENERAL EDITOR'S PREFACE

This, the fifteenth volume of *Suffolk Charters*, is edited by Dr Richard Mortimer, who produced the very first volume in 1979 and was coeditor of the next three. The Society is most grateful to him for returning to the fold to edit a series of original documents which are now in his custody in his capacity of Archivist to the Dean and Chapter of Westminster.

The next volume in the series will be another collection of original charters, those of Dodnash Priory. Work is proceeding on other volumes, including the Suffolk nunneries, the vill of Stanton, the Tollemache family, the Pakenham family and Ixworth priory, and St Peter and St Paul, Ipswich.

The Society and the general editor are extremely grateful for continued support for volumes edited by London graduates from Isobel Thornley's Bequest to the University of London, and in particular to the Secretary of the committee, Miss Pat Crimmin, for facilitating this assistance. The Society is also indebted to Boydell and Brewer, and especially to Dr Richard Barber, for their careful work in the production of the series.

*Christopher Harper-Bill*

This volume is published with the assistance of
a grant from Isobel Thornley's Bequest to
the University of London

# ACKNOWLEDGEMENTS

This book, which was originally accepted for the Series by the late R. Allen Brown, has been a long time in the making, and I should like to thank the General Editor, Christopher Harper-Bill, for his forbearance as well as for his comments. My thanks are also due to Barbara Harvey for valuable discussion and help on many matters, to Edward Martin of the Suffolk County Council Planning Department for help with listed buildings, and to Bill and Sandra Martin for their hospitality in and around Sudbury. I am especially grateful to Christine Reynolds and Tony Trowles for their patience with a partly absent and often absent-minded colleague. Richard Barber and the staff of Boydell and Brewer have acted throughout with their customary efficiency. I am grateful to the British Library for permission to publish two documents from the Cottonian cartulary of Westminster abbey.

*Richard Mortimer*                                    Westminster Abbey Muniment Room

# ABBREVIATIONS

| | |
|---|---|
| *Aug Friars* | *The Cartulary of the Augustinian Friars of Clare*, ed. C. Harper-Bill, Suffolk Charters Series xi, 1991 |
| BL | British Library |
| *Cal Ch R* | *Calendar of Charter Rolls*, HMSO, London, 1903– |
| *Cal Inq PM* | *Calendar of Inquisitions Post Mortem*, 16 vols., London 1917 etc. |
| *Cal Pap Letters* | *Calendar of Papal Letters*, 14 vols., London 1894 etc. |
| *Cal Pat R* | *Calendar of Patent Rolls*, HMSO, London, 1891– |
| *CRR* | *Curia Regis Rolls*, 16 vols., London 1923 etc. |
| DB | Domesday Book |
| DNB | Dictionary of National Biography |
| Dodwell, *Fines* | *Feet of Fines for the County of Norfolk (1202–15) and of Suffolk (1199–1214)*, Pipe Roll Society n.s. xxxii (1958) |
| *Essex Fines* | *Feet of Fines for Essex* i, ed. R.E.G. and E.F. Kirk, Colchester 1899; ii, ed. R.E.G. Kirk, Colchester 1913 |
| *Exc e Rot Fin* | *Excerpta e Rotulis Finium*, ed. C. Roberts, 2 vols., Record Commission, London 1835–6 |
| *Fasti i* | *John le Neve, Fasti Ecclesiae Anglicanae 1066–1300 i, St Pauls*, ed. Diana E. Greenway, London 1968 |
| *Kal Sam* | *The Kalendar of Abbot Samson of Bury St Edmunds and Related Documents*, ed. R.H.C. Davis, Camden Third Series lxxxiv, London 1954 |
| Hodson, 'St Bartholomew's' | W.W. Hodson, 'Saint Bartholomew's Priory, Sudbury', *Proceedings of the Suffolk Institute of Archaeology and Natural History* 7, 1891, 17–22 |
| *Mon Ang* | William Dugdale, *Monasticon Anglicanum*, ed. J. Caley, H. Ellis and B. Bandinel, 6 vols., London 1817–30 |
| *Monks* | E.H. Pearce, *The Monks of Westminster*, Cambridge 1916 |
| *Norwich Acta* | *English Episcopal Acta vi, Norwich 1070–1214*, ed. Christopher Harper-Bill, Oxford 1990 |
| *PR* | Pipe Roll |
| PRO | Public Record Office |
| *Red Bk* | *The Red Book of the Exchequer*, ed. Hubert Hall, Rolls Series, London 1896 |
| *Rot Cur Reg* | *Rotuli Curiae Regis*, ed. Francis Palgrave, 2 vols., 1835 |

| | |
|---|---|
| *RRAN* | *Regesta Regum Anglo-Normannorum*, vol. ii, ed. C. Johnson and H.A. Cronne, Oxford 1956 |
| Rye, *Fines* | *A Calendar of the Feet of Fines for Suffolk*, ed. Walter Rye, Ipswich 1900 |
| Sperling | C.F.D. Sperling, *A Short History of the Borough of Sudbury in the County of Suffolk*, Sudbury 1896 |
| *Stoke by Clare* | *Stoke by Clare Cartulary*, ed. Christopher Harper-Bill and Richard Mortimer, 3 vols., Suffolk Charters Series iv–vi, Woodbridge 1982–4 |
| *Taxatio* | *Taxatio ecclesiastica Angliae et Walliae auctoritate P. Nicholai IV*, ed. J. Caley and J. Hunter, 6 vols., Record Commission, 1810–34 |
| *Valor* | *Valor Ecclesiasticus*, Record Commission, 1810 |
| VCH | Victoria County History |
| WAM | Westminster Abbey Muniments |

# PRIORS AND OTHER HEADS OF THE HOUSE[1]

| | |
|---|---|
| Brian | occ. 1222 (*Essex Fines* i, 62) |
| Gilbert | mid-13th century (nos 7, 9–10, 26; cf. no. 20) |
| John of Rickmansworth | mid-13th century (nos 8, 11, 22, 97) |
| Richard de Dol | occ. 1279 (no. 106), 1282 (no. 31), 1283–5 (nos 112, 115–6) |
| Gregory | late 13th century (nos 60, 104) |
| Henry of London | late 13th century (nos 27, 34) |
| Nicholas of Ware | occ. –1286 (no. 38), 1303 (nos 89–90) |
| Simon | occ. 1299 (no. 35), 1300 (no. 37) |
| Roger de Buiyns | dead by 28 January 1310 (*Cal Pap Letters* ii, 65) |
| Simon de Henlegh | occ. 1323 (nos 44–5) |
| Thomas Flete | appointed 1499 (no. 131) |

1 See below, p. 5.

# LIST OF MANUSCRIPTS

Westminster Abbey Muniments

| | | |
|---|---|---|
| 20759 = 2 | 20797 = 107 | 20836 = 74 |
| 20760 = 59 | 20798 = 108 | 20837 = 28 |
| 20761 = 3 | 20799 = 109 | 20838 = 25 |
| 20762 = 91 | 20800 = 110 | 20839 = 72 |
| 20763 = 122 | 20801 = 111 | 20840 = 73 |
| 20764 = " | 20802 = 112 | 20841 = 71 |
| 20765 = 123 | 20803 = 113 | 20842 = 11 |
| 20766 = 14 | 20804 = 114 | 20843 = 19 |
| 20767 = 4 | 20805 = 115 | 20844 = 66 |
| 20768 = 124 | 20806 = 116 | 20845 = 75 |
| 20769 = 23 | 20807 = 117 | 20846 = 40 |
| 20770 = 42 | 20808 = 118 | 20847 = 41 |
| 20771 = 20 | 20809 = 119 | 20848 = 44 |
| 20772 = 43 | 20810 = 96 | 20849 = 45 |
| 20773 = 5 | 20811 = 36 | 20850 = 97 |
| 20774 = 100 | 20812 = 37 | 20851 = 8 |
| 20775 = 104 | 20813 = 37 | 20852 = 80 |
| 20776 = 12 | 20814 = 87 | 20853 = 81 |
| 20777 = 24 | 20815 = 88 | 20854 = 70 |
| 20778 = 60 | 20816 = 35 | 20855 = 27 |
| 20779 = 6 | 20817 = 85 | 20856 = 98 |
| 20780 = 15 | 20818 = 125 | 20857 = 89 |
| 20781 = 92 | 20820 = 93 | 20858 = 38 |
| 20782 = 77 | 20821 = 30 | 20859 = 39 |
| 20783 = 67 | 20822 = 82 | 20860 = 69 |
| 20784 = 16 | 20823 = 86 | 20861 = 79 |
| 20785 = 7 | 20824 = 26 | 20862 = 78 |
| 20786 = 21 | 20825 = 84 | 20863 = 90 |
| 20787 = 101 | 20826 = 83 | 20864 = 99 |
| 20788 = 17 | 20827 = 33 | 20865 = 46 |
| 20789 = 9 | 20828 = 94 | 20866 = 47 |
| 20790 = 10 | 20829 = 68 | 20867 = 48 & 126 |
| 20791 = 18 | 20830 = 102 | 20868 = 49 |
| 20792 = 13 | 20831 = 29 | 20869 = 50 |
| 20793 = 63 | 20832 = 61 | 20870 = 51 |
| 20794 = 31 | 20833 = 22 | 20871 = 52 |
| 20795 = 105 | 20834 = 76 | 20872 = 53 |
| 20796 = 106 | 20835 = 95 | 20873 = 54 |

| | | |
|---|---|---|
| 20874 = 55 | 20880 = 130 | 20885 = 62 |
| 20875 = 65 | 20881 = 34 | 20886 = 58 |
| 20876 = 56 | 20882 = 129 | 20887 = 131 |
| 20877 = 127 | 20883 = 57 | 22836 = 64 |
| 20878 = 128 | 20884 = 120 | 22859 = 121 |
| 20879 = 32 | | |

British Library

Cotton Faustina A ii, fo 79r–v 1
                     fo 79v    103

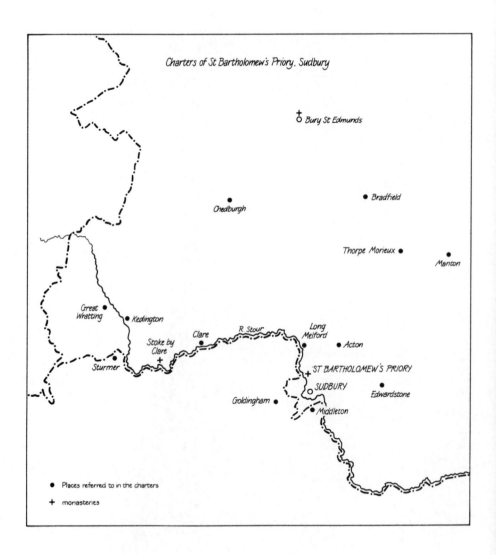

Charters of St Bartholomew's Priory, Sudbury

✝
○ Bury St Edmunds

● Bradfield

● Chedburgh

Thorpe Morieux ●

● Manton

Great
Wratting ●
● Kedington

Clare ●     R. Stour

Long
Melford
✝

● Acton

Stoke by
Clare
✝

'ST BARTHOLOMEW'S PRIORY

Sturmer ●

SUDBURY
○

Edwardstone ●

Goldingham ●

● Middleton

● Places referred to in the charters

✝ monasteries

# INTRODUCTION

*History*

The priory of St Bartholomew, Sudbury, is probably the poorest and most obscure institution so far to have attracted the attention of the Suffolk Charters Series. Very little has ever appeared in print about it, even the *Victoria County History* ignoring its existence.[1] The most remarkable fact about it is that it has left a group of original charters among the muniments of Westminster abbey, of which it was a cell. They shed a good deal of light on its history and possessions, all the more interesting for illuminating such a small institution. Cells like St Bartholomew's are usually regarded as a source of weakness to the monastic body as a whole, centres of indiscipline too small to have a proper common life and too distant to be supervised.[2] Certainly by the later fourteenth century Westminster abbey was sufficiently disenchanted with the possession of St Bartholomew's that it attempted to exchange the estate there for lucrative and more easily managed property in the city of London. Nevertheless the charters show that St Bartholomew's had a period of energy and expansion in the thirteenth century: even if it did not attract significant pious gifts after the early thirteenth century – with one remarkable exception a century later – it had the energy to expand and consolidate its lands, and had money to spend on doing so. It is this phase that most of the surviving charters illustrate.

St Bartholomew's priory next to Sudbury was founded as a cell of Westminster abbey by Wulfric the moneyer at some time before 1116. His gift was in return for fraternity and admission as a monk, apparently at St Bartholomew's itself. The property had been the subject of litigation in the king's court, but why or between whom is not known; Henry I's charter, which is the earliest in the priory's archive, is a confirmation of St Bartholomew's to Westminster after this litigation (no. 1). Wulfric is known from surviving coins as a Sudbury moneyer in the time of William the Conqueror, William II and Henry I;[3] it seems likely that the gift was made at the end of Wulfric's career, perhaps not long before 1116. Nothing can be recovered with certainty about his life beyond these bare facts. Wulfric was a common name, and there may have been other contemporary moneyers who bore it; we cannot know whether he worked in other places besides Sudbury. Though there was more than one

---

[1] VCH *Suffolk* ii, 150–2 confuses St Bartholomew's with the priory of Edwardstone, even though the latter is correctly described (ii, 76) as a cell of Abingdon later moved to Colne in Essex; Hodson, 'St Bartholomew's', repeated almost verbatim in Sperling, 176–9.

[2] D. Knowles, *The Monastic Order in England*, Cambridge 1949, 136, 433, 686–7.

[3] He is known to have made coins of William I types VI and VIII, William II types II and perhaps V, and Henry I types III and V: G.C. Brooke, *Catalogue of English Coins in the British Museum. Norman Kings*, 2 vols, London 1916, i, ccxl–ccxli.

moneyer at Sudbury in 1086,[4] the mint there was not particularly important: it was 'much smaller and more occasional' than those of Thetford and Norwich.[5] Westminster was perhaps not an obvious place for a would-be monastic entrant living in west Suffolk to turn to. The choice of a monastery near London might be explained by Wulfric's profession. The dies from which he struck coins were very probably made in London, entailing a journey to London to collect them, giving him the opportunity to observe the monastic community at Westminster, which from c.1085 to 1117 or 1118 flourished under one of its most distinguished abbots, Gilbert Crispin. It was in his time that most or all of Westminster's cells were founded.[6]

The first mention of St Bartholomew's after Henry I's confirmation charter is a perplexing reference in a bull of Pope Adrian IV, datable to 1157. This confirms Westminster's cells as possessions of the mother house, including the *cellula* of St Bartholomew, with the church of St Gregory, Sudbury.[7] There is no other indication that St Gregory's ever belonged to Westminster or St Bartholomew's. It is not mentioned in Henry I's confirmation (no. 1), and in the 1150s it was given, along with its chapel of St Peter, by William, earl of Gloucester to the nunnery of Nuneaton in Warwickshire.[8] Nuneaton continued to hold the right of presentation to St Gregory's until Simon Thebaud acquired it from the nuns in order to found a college of secular priests there in 1375.[9] St Gregory's was the main church in Sudbury and was well endowed, having been a minster in Anglo-Saxon times, to which land was left by will in the tenth century.[10] Relations with it are a leading theme in the history of St Bartholomew's. It is clear from the tithe dispute with the rector in 1323 that the ancient possessions of St Bartholomew's were not tithed, in effect putting the cell outside the parish (nos 42–5), a situation which continued down to the nineteenth century. This situation was old in 1323; twelfth-century landowners are often found granting their tithe away from the parish church to a monastic foundation, and Henry I's confirmation charter specifies tithes along with St Bartholomew's other possessions and privileges. Its separate ecclesiastical status therefore goes back to Wulfric's time.

The history of St Bartholomew's is soon told. It would seem that there was a fire there in the early thirteenth century, since the abbot of Westminster offered fraternity to those who contributed to the house's repair (no. 124). The thirteenth century was the heyday of the acquisition of further lands under Priors Gilbert and Gregory, and John of Rickmansworth; it was also agitated by the long-running dispute over the tithes of Thorpe Morieux, the house's second most valuable endowment.[11] Ivo of Thorpe had given two parts of the tithes of his demesne lands at a date some time before 1135, since Henry II's charter

---

[4] DB, fo 286b.

[5] C.E. Challis, *A New History of the Royal Mint*, Cambridge 1992, 64.

[6] J. Armitage Robinson, *Gilbert Crispin Abbot of Westminster*, Cambridge 1911, 32–4.

[7] Walther Holtzmann, *Papsturkunden in England*, 3 vols, Berlin 1930, i, 325; WAM Book 11 ('Domesday' cartulary), fo 4v.

[8] *Norwich Acta* no. 136, Bishop William Turbe's confirmation c.1159 × 1166; William was styled earl from 1153.

[9] Dodwell, *Fines* no. 464; BL Add. Ch. 47967; VCH *Suffolk* ii, 150.

[10] P.H. Sawyer, *Anglo-Saxon Charters*, London 1968, nos 1486, 1501.

[11] See below, and nos 105–18.

confirming the gift refers to a charter of his grandfather Henry I which has not survived (no. 103). This kind of grant was often commuted for an annual pension by the late thirteenth century. In Westminster's view, the rector of Thorpe was withholding their tithes (no. 108), and the difficulty was to get the rector or his proctors into court. The case dragged on, prolonged by 'multiple contumacy and frivolous appeals' (no. 116); the excommunication of the rector did not end it. Perhaps the assessment of the tithes of Thorpe belonging to St Bartholomew's in 1291 at £1[12] implies that a settlement was eventually reached.

Tithes caused another dispute which has left its mark on the documents, with Mr Warin of Fulbourn, rector of St Gregory's. The result was an agreement specifying the non-titheable possessions of St Bartholomew's, the monks conceding tithe from some of their land (no. 44) and coming to an agreement about lands particularly in dispute (no. 45). The dossier contains two interesting informal pieces (nos 42–3) recording some of the discussions leading up to the presentation of Westminster's case. There was another such lawsuit with St Gregory's, by then a collegiate church, in 1418, which has left only one document (no. 58).

Perhaps the greatest event in the priory's history was the foundation of the Thebaud chantry. This was the work of Nigel Thebaud, son of Nigel and brother of the Mr Simon Thebaud, alias Simon of Sudbury, who later became one of Sudbury's most eminent sons. Simon entered the church, became a papal chaplain and was much used in diplomacy between England and the papal court. In 1349 he was given a canonry at Hereford cathedral, in 1353 one at Salisbury, and in 1361 he was made bishop of London. During these years he seems to have continued the life of a peripatetic diplomat, and was not consecrated as bishop until March 1362. In 1375 he was translated to Canterbury, and in 1381 was murdered by the rebels of the Peasants' Revolt on Tower Hill. It was when he was bishop of London that he acquired the advowson of St Gregory's, and founded the college of secular priests to serve it and St Peter's. The charters concerning the chantry foundation at St Bartholomew's permit the following reconstruction:

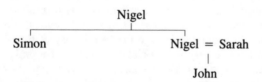

No 47 makes it clear that Simon was the brother, not as has often been stated the son, of the Nigel Thebaud who was married to one Sarah.[13] Simon's father was in all probability dead by 1345 when Simon quitclaimed to his brother all the land his father gave him (no. 47). Nigel, Simon's brother, was dead by 1357 when his son John quitclaimed his rights in the 80 acres which became the endowment of the chantry (no. 54). The foundation process began in May 1349,

[12] See below, p. 7.
[13] VCH *Suffolk* ii, 150; DNB; *Mon Ang* vi, 1370; R.C. Fowler (ed.), *Registrum Simonis de Sudbiria*, Canterbury and York Society, Oxford 1927, v.

just as the Black Death was at its height, when Nigel Thebaud conveyed 80 acres to a group of feoffees including some local clergymen and Richard Rook, a citizen of Westminster (no. 49), and Abbot Simon de Bircheston of Westminster granted the prayers of the house, including a daily mass at St Bartholomew's, to the donors (no. 48). The abbot's document includes Elizabeth de Burgh, Lady of Clare, among the beneficiaries, probably because she was also the lady of Sudbury and presumably consented to the transaction – she is not known to have made any grants to St Bartholomew's or Westminster. Two of the feoffees of no. 49, one of them John Thebaud, subsequently resigned their rights to Richard Rook (nos 52, 54), and it was Rook who finally, in 1357, made the grant of the land to the abbot and prior for the souls of Nigel and his relatives (no. 55). At this period it was necessary to acquire a licence in mortmain in order to grant land to the church, and it was not until 1 May 1361 that such a licence was issued.[14] This probably explains the creation of another deed of grant by Richard Rook, dated a few months after the licence, to regularize the position (no. 56). A grant of land to some of the feoffees by Mariota le Dextere, and a quitclaim by her son (nos 50–1) may represent a stage in the acquisition of the eighty acres, or it could be a separate grant.

This very substantial addition to the endowment does not seem to have ensured the priory's future. It seems ironic that within a few years a papal indulgence was issued to those granting alms to St Bartholomew's, because of the alleged insufficiency of its means (nos 127–8). Within thirty years of the Thebaud gift, Westminster abbey was making serious moves to rid itself of St Bartholomew's by an exchange with the new college of St Gregory's. Westminster was to receive a messuage and three shops in the city of London, which Simon of Sudbury had bought when bishop of London and given to his foundation; in return St Gregory's was to have the entire estate of St Bartholomew's. A licence in mortmain was obtained for the transfer in 1380.[15] The abbot's deed granting the priory was executed in February 1382 (no. 129), after the archbishop had been murdered; it is not known why the agreement did not take effect. It is nevertheless striking that Westminster should have been ready to dispose of St Bartholomew's so completely. The archbishop would have been passing on to his new foundation land that his brother had given as a family chantry. Nigel and Sarah Thebaud were buried in St Gregory's,[16] and it no doubt seemed appropriate and convenient to change the beneficiary of their gift.

The priory's later history is completely obscure. The only indication of its continued monastic status is Abbot Fascet's appointment in 1499 of an elderly monk, Thomas Flete, as prior for life, as a kind of retirement (no. 131). Not to be confused with John Flete the chronicler, Thomas Flete had been a monk for thirty years, had briefly been archdeacon, and had been custodian of the Lady Chapel for the last ten years. For some of that time he had also been kitchener.[17]

Monastic life must have come to an end by 1536, for on 22 February of that year the whole site of the priory was let by the abbot and convent of Westminster

14 *Cal Pat R* 1361–4, 11.
15 *Cal Pat R* 1377–81, 552.
16 Sperling, 105–6.
17 *Monks*, 163.

to William Butt of London.[18] This is the earliest of a nearly continuous series of leases going down to the nineteenth century recorded in the abbey lease books. The chapel continued as such, Westminster abbey paying the stipend of a curate to celebrate divine service there, as recorded in the *Valor Ecclesiasticus*, right down to the nineteenth century.[19]

Such information as we possess about the internal life of the priory shows no more than a pair of monks and their prior in residence at any one time. In 1189–90 Brothers Robert of Clare and Martin were serving God at St Bartholomew's, and in the early thirteenth century there were Brothers Alan and John under Brother Gilbert the *procurator* (nos 2, 20). Gilbert was also referred to as prior (no. 7). He was followed by John of Rickmansworth, who dealt with Petronilla, widow of Nicholas of Colchester (no. 11); Gilbert had dealt with her husband (e.g. no. 7). The endorsement of no. 8 proves that 'Prior John' was John of Rickmansworth; he was probably also the Prior John of no. 97.

In the later thirteenth century the succession becomes more confused. The only fixed point in the sequence is Prior Simon, who occurs in 1299 and 1300 (nos 35, 37). Richard de Dol was involved in the purchase of a meadow in 1282 (no. 31), in between appearances as proctor for Westminster abbey in the lawsuit about the tithes of Thorpe Morieux in 1279 and 1283–5 (nos 106, 112, 115, 116); though he is nowhere called prior, it seems likely that he was in charge of the cell's interests in these years. Nicholas of Ware has to be fitted in somehow; he occurs both before 1286 (no. 38) and probably in 1303 (nos 89–90). It is not impossible that one man may have had two spells as prior; or it could be that when he was involved in the acquisition of nos 89 and 90 he was not the titular head of the house; or again, there could have been two men of the same name. Priors Gregory (nos 60, 104) and Henry of London (nos 27, 34) also have to be accommodated. The 'J. de Wenlac' who acquired no. 32 may have been John of Wenlock, a known Westminster monk, but he is not described as prior. Simon de Henlegh, 'prior or *custos*' in 1323 (nos 44–5), had had a long career at Westminster: he was chamberlain from 1298 to 1304, which proves that he was not the Prior Simon of 1299–1300.[20] Two priors are known from judicial and papal documents, but have left no trace in the charters: Brian of 1222, and Roger de Buiyns who was dead by 28 January 1310.[21]

It is noticeable that the topographical names of known monks are not local, but are places in the vicinity of Westminster such as Rickmansworth (Herts.) or from which other monks of Westminster had come – Abbots Richard of Ware and Walter of Wenlock, for instance. The twelfth-century Robert of Clare (no. 2) is an exception. But there probably was some local recruitment: Richard of Kedington, also known as Richard of Sudbury, occurs as a Westminster monk from 1303, and was elected abbot in 1308. The otherwise unknown Prior Roger de Buiyns objected, on the grounds that he had not been summoned to take part in the election.[22] There was a large party at Westminster opposed to Richard's

---

[18] WAM Lease Book ii, for 315r.
[19] *Valor* i, 411; WAM 39009 etc.; Hodson, 'St Bartholomew's', 21.
[20] *Monks*, 68.
[21] See list of priors, above, p. xii.
[22] *Cal Pap Letters* ii, 65.

election including another probable Suffolk monk, Roger of Bures.[23] The handful of monks at St Bartholomew's was headed and replenished by monks from the mother house, but might also attract some local recruits who went on to Westminster.[24]

The little cell was completely subject to Westminster – with so few monks and such a slender income it could never have been self-sustaining. Its monks were clearly monks of Westminster. Prior Flete in effect retired to St Bartholomew's, and it looks as if Simon de Henlegh may have done so nearly two centuries earlier. Prior Brian was unable to plead in the king's court on his own account in 1222, and unable to conclude a final concord except in the presence and with the consent of the abbot of Westminster. Nevertheless the cell seems to have had some practical autonomy, especially in the thirteenth century, running its own business and acquiring land with its own money.

The late fourteenth-century inventory (no. 130) provides our only glimpse of daily life inside the little priory. The chapel had all it needed, including a relic of St Bartholomew, but nothing that sounds very grand. The living quarters consisted of a hall and chamber, with a kitchen, larder, bakehouse and barn. In the chamber the prior had his table and the servants theirs, with bronze candlesticks, a tin salt-cellar and a pepper mill. The equipment in the bakehouse, with its large vats, implies that the monks brewed their own beer as well as baking their own bread. There were a few liturgical books, but nothing that seems personal: monks at this period had wages and personal property, so the inventory presumably catalogues the cell's possessions rather than those of its inhabitants.

Two of the medieval buildings are still standing: the chapel and the barn, the former also currently used as a barn. Both are listed ancient monuments. The chapel is a rectangular structure of flint rubble with diagonal corner buttresses and one buttress in the centre of each long side, 53 feet by 19 feet,[25] a single cell in plan. It is dated to the early fifteenth century in the listing schedule, and has four-centred arches of Tudor type over the east and west windows. While an early fifteenth-century date is not impossible – nothing, after all, is known of the priory's history in that period – a date in the mid-fourteenth century, after the foundation of the Thebaud chantry, would fit better with what we know of its history. St Bartholomew's is probably the only monastic foundation in Suffolk of which the church survives complete and roofed. The barn, one of the finest in the county, is dated to the fourteenth century. It is an aisled six-bay structure with two threshing floors, timber-framed and weatherboarded, with a thatched roof. The roof is probably seventeenth-century.[26] Again, a fourteenth-century date goes well with the expansion of the priory's agriculture consequent on the Thebaud gift. It is in all likelihood the barn of which the contents are inventoried in no. 130. The domestic quarters have disappeared. The present farmhouse dates from the mid- or late sixteenth century with later alterations and additions.

---

[23] *Monks*, 73–4.

[24] The locative names are not always reliable: see Barbara Harvey, *Living and Dying in England 1100–1540*, Oxford 1993, 75–6.

[25] Dimensions given in Hodson, 'St Bartholomew's', 21, chapel illustrated opp. p. 17.

[26] Listing schedule, Suffolk County Planning Department.

*Possessions*

The endowment consisted of a home farm surrounding the priory's buildings, and a small quantity of rents in and around Sudbury, with a tithe from lands in Thorpe Morieux. The *Taxatio Ecclesiastica* of Pope Nicholas IV (1291) assesses the value of the priory's possessions at £3 3s 4d from lands and rents in the parish of St Gregory's, Sudbury, 4s 2d rent in St Peter's parish, 3s rent in Acton, and the portion of tithes at Thorpe Morieux at £1: total, £4 10s 6d. This source may underestimate the actual value, and it omits any mention of income from Melford, for instance, where the priory certainly had some land, however little; but it provides a comparison with the most valuable of Sudbury's churches, St Gregory's, which is valued at £16 13s 4d.[27] St Bartholomew's was certainly a small, poor foundation.

Most of the priory's lands therefore lay in the fields of Sudbury, in St Gregory's parish; details can be gained from the tithe agreement of 1323 with the rector of St Gregory's (no. 44) which in effect lists the monks' lands in the parish. The total holding comes to 122½ acres of land and 12¼ acres of meadow. Our next glimpse of the priory's endowment comes in the 1380s, when Abbot Litlington's grant of the priory to St Gregory's College (no. 129) repeats exactly the details given in a mortmain licence of 1380 sanctioning the exchange between Westminster Abbey and St Gregory's of the priory's estate in return for buildings and shops in the city of London.[28] In these two documents the priory is described as comprising a messuage (the priory buildings), 210 acres of arable land, 1½ acres of meadow, 15 acres of pasture, and rents of 23s, 1 pound of pepper, 4½ quarters of wheat, a cock, a hen and a boon-work in autumn, in the vills of Sudbury, Long Melford, Bulmer, Acton, Middleton, Cavendish, Brundon, Edwardstone and Thorpe Morieux. The endowment was held in chief of the king except for 80 acres. These 80 acres must have been those granted in 1349 to endow the Thebaud chantry (no. 49): the land was in Holgate, adjoining land already owned by St Bartholomew's, and was held of 'the chief lord of the fee', who was not named.

The *Valor Ecclesiasticus* of Henry VIII's reign is a disappointing source in regard to the priory's property, which is described as worth £10, and no further details given.[29] More useful is a terrier of 1552 listing the names of pieces of land and giving their acreage: the total is 128½ acres, including 10½ acres of meadow and pasture, all in the vicinity of what was still called 'the howse and pryory of bartholmewys'.[30]

In the late nineteenth century W.W. Hodson knew of a map of 1656, which he describes: this time the total is given as 180 acres and a number of field names is supplied.[31] The St Bartholomew's estate continued as a possession of Westminster abbey, in the hands of a succession of lessees, and in 1802 one J. Prickett made a survey of it, accompanied by a map.[32] The total quantity of land

27 *Taxatio*, 122a, 133a–b.
28 *Cal Pat R* 1377–81, 552.
29 *Valor* i, 411.
30 WAM 20889.
31 Hodson, 'St Bartholomew's', 21.
32 WAM Ch. Comm. Deed 146088, Map 12577.

was 180 acres 2 roods 14 perches, and all consolidated in the area of the priory except an outlying piece of meadow called Bartholomew's Mead in Lolham Meadow, and a piece at Bulmer which was not mapped.

The priory's endowment of land around its own buildings was thus very stable from at least the early fourteenth century to the Reformation and even down to the nineteenth century. The 122½ acres of arable in St Gregory's parish of 1323 must be more or less the 130 acres left when the 80 acres acquired in 1349 are subtracted from the 210 acres mentioned in 1380. The 12¼ acres of meadow of 1323, with the addition of meadow in other places, would produce the 16½ acres of meadow and pasture of 1380. In 1552 the figures are 118½ acres of arable and 10½ acres of meadow, considerably down from the 210 acres of 1380. In 1656 and 1802 the estate comprised about 180 acres. Some of the discrepancies might be due to differences in measurement: the 1323 quantities are given 'by common estimation', not the result of measuring (nos 43, 45), but even in the nineteenth century surveyors could produce different results – a pencil note on the 1802 map mentions that a measurement in 1847 showed 185 acres. It is also clear that ownership in the fields had evolved in detail, which is not surprising over so long a period. The land acquired in Sudbury represented by the twelfth- and thirteenth-century charters adds up to only 26¼ acres and two acres of meadow. It is thus very likely that the original endowment from the time of Wulfric was the basic nucleus of the estate, rounded off and slightly increased by purchase in the thirteenth century and then considerably expanded by the acquisition of 80 acres as the endowment of the Thebaud chantry in the mid-fourteenth century.

With such a small endowment there is little to say about the monks' estate management. A piece of land, probably small, in Holgate was let out in 1299 (no. 37), and Prior Gregory let the land in Thorpe Morieux on a lifetime lease (no. 104). Otherwise the priory seems to have run its land as a farm, presumably living off the produce and selling the surplus. The prior's animals were grazing in *Setecopp'* field before 1323 (no. 45). The inventory shows that in the late fourteenth century, a period when the larger institutions leased their demesnes, St Bartholomew's still maintained its farm, with a small quantity of livestock – only two cows and two sheep – but a fair amount of grain, mostly barley, oats and wheat and also pulses (no. 130). The sale of surplus produce is the most likely explanation for the sums of money of which the thirteenth-century priors disposed, and with which they bought land. Here the annual gifts of grain from early pious donors must have come in useful, helping to maintain supplies in poor farming years.[33] On one occasion (no. 20) the monks bought out controverted rights with a gift of grain, which proves that there was a disposable surplus, at least in some years. The monks had been given by charter the right to have their malt ground at Brundon mill. In 1222 Prior Brian complained that Roger de Manant was not honouring this gift and sued Roger, who eventually agreed to grind all the corn for making bread for the monks' table before anyone else's except his own and without taking a toll.[34] As well as the home farm the monks had tenants: a list of

[33] See below, p. 10.
[34] *Essex Fines* i, 62.

them has survived from the late thirteenth century, unfortunately mostly illegible.[35]

The 1323 agreement reveals a landscape which combines large single fields such as *Hipemere*, 40 acres and more, and much smaller pieces, perhaps enclosed, like *Ridelescroft*, 4½ acres, the 5-acre *Florelond*, and all 2½ acres of *Copehod*. It is also clear that other people owned pieces interpersed with the monks' land, such as William de Malton's and Nigel Thebaud's pieces. Many of the charters which are phrased as grants to the priory were really sales, as the priory gave money in return. These sums are described as given *in gersuma*, a phrase for which there is no equivalent in modern English; it is in effect the purchase price. Many of the thirteenth-century charters show the gradual acquisition by the monks of such pieces described as between and next to their own land. The result, and no doubt the aim, of this process would be consolidation. Some charters show laymen doing the same: Nicholas Ording's acquisitions in Kedington are often described as lying next to his own land (e.g. nos 71–3). The priory's advantage was that it was an undying institution, which could reap where Nicholas Ording had sown. There is no record of Parliamentary enclosure. None was necessary – enclosure had been all but reached over the centuries without it.

An element of continuity is provided by the field names, some of which were the same in 1552, 1656 and 1802 – Pond Field (*the Ponde Fyllde*), St Bartholomew's Field (*Bartholomewefylld*) by the Sudbury-Melford road, Furzey Field (*Furssy paster*), and Lolham Meadow (*Lowllam medow*). Some sixteenth-century names had been lost, or at least were not marked on the 1802 map – *Hoddefylde*, *Pryors fylde*, *Browmehyle* for instance – and apparently new names acquired (Dove House Field, Rye Hill, Battledoor Piece, etc.). But some later names went back to the middle ages. King's Wood Hill and King's Wood Field on the 1802 map represent the Kingswood of the charters, a name going back at least to the twelfth century when it was still a wood (no. 2). It is also likely that the Great and Little Fair Fields of 1802, on either side of the lane leading to the Sudbury-Melford road, are the 'two pieces of land called *Feirelond*', comprising 14 acres, before the west gate of the priory in 1323 (no. 44). It could be that the twelfth-century *Hiopemere* (no. 2), the fourteenth-century *Hipemere* (nos 44–5), is represented in 1656 and 1802 by Hickmoore Field. North Meadow, which occurs in 1349 (no. 49) and the 1802 map, is still a feature of Sudbury today. Thus larger pieces of land, such as the Fair Fields, and prominent features like Kingswood and the North Meadow, retain their name over many centuries and provide a topographical framework, as the roads in all probability do as well, within which small adjustments took place.

## The charters

The 131 documents printed here, 129 from originals in the muniments of Westminster abbey, consist overwhelmingly of thirteenth-century deeds. Only seven are twelfth-century (nos 1, 2, 59, 64, possibly 91, 103, 122); 34 are fourteenth-century (nos 35, 40–57, 65, 85–90, 120, 125–30 and possibly

[35] WAM 20819.

no. 32). The earliest dated document, apart from no. 2 of 1189–90, is of 1279 (nos 105–6). The difficulty of assigning a date to the undated deeds of the thirteenth century is usually lightened by references to individual people in the public records, but unfortunately most of the people occurring in these charters are too obscure to figure there. Most of the documents have had to be given vague 'early' or 'late' thirteenth-century dates, meaning no more than the first or second half of the century, with 'mid thirteenth-century' used equally vaguely for those from the middle third.

Some of the groups of documents have been mentioned under the history of the priory: those from the disputes about the tithes of Thorpe Morieux and of the priory's lands in Sudbury (nos 105–18, 42–5), and the various deeds of the Thebaud gift (nos 47–56). The charters reveal that the priory attracted very little in the way of pious gifts from the lesser inhabitants of the region. Such as there were seem to have come in during the twelfth and early thirteenth centuries, notably the gifts of grain by a group of local lords. The earliest among these is probably the measure of wheat granted by Hugh de Montchensy about the middle of the twelfth century: he also confirmed a similar gift by his tenant William of Goldingham (no. 64). Roger de St German, lord of Cavendish, granted a further measure in the late twelfth century (no. 122), and Bartholomew of Baylham half a measure perhaps a little later (no. 91). Two further grants of grain, by Roger de Montchensy and Hugh de Collingham, are not represented by surviving charters, and are known only from a later confirmation by the bishop of Norwich (no. 125); the bishop confirms a total of 4½ *summe*, which were still part of the priory's income in 1382 (no. 129) – a *summa*, or measure, equals one quarter. Of the few charitable grants of land, the most generous were those of three acres near Kingswood by Osbert son of Richard in the early thirteenth century (no. 17), and 2½ acres in Acton which Robert *Magister* gave to secure his burial at St Bartholomew's (no. 59). Another twelfth-century pious gift is that of nearly 1½ acres by John son of Benedict, also near Kingswood (no. 2).

The great majority of the other charters represent purchases of small pieces of land by the monks, mostly in the fields surrounding their house, during the course of the thirteenth century. Such were the 1½ acres sold by Nicholas of Colchester from the dowry of his wife Petronilla (no. 6). The family can be reconstructed as follows:

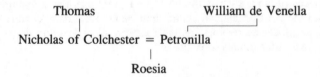

All together Priors Gilbert and John acquired 3 acres probably of Petronilla's dowry and 7 acres left to Roesia by her grandfather William de Venella in the vicinity of the priory for a total of 19 marks plus 1s rent, and 2½ acres of Petronilla's land in Melford for 4½ marks (nos 6–11, 97).

The priory also bought 5 acres of arable land and one acre of meadow to supplement what appears to have been a grant of 3 acres, from Osbert son of

Richard, probably the father-in-law of Michael the mayor (nos 13–20).[36] The price paid for the meadow, 3s, seems very cheap, since the arable was sold for over one mark (13s 4d) per acre, so there may have been a charitable element in the sale. The documents include quitclaims from Osbert's two daughters and their husbands: there had been a lawsuit between the priory and Osbert's daughter Margaret and her husband William le Fatte about Margaret's rights in the land, which the priory had to buy out with a gift of grain (no. 20).

But the most striking group of charters in the collection is those of Nicholas Ording, who put together an estate in Kedington and vicinity which his son Richard eventually gave to the priory. The family can be charted as follows (nos 66, 69, 70, 78, 87–8):

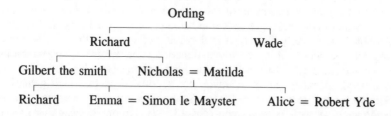

The charters show the gradual purchase of land in and around Kedington. Richard son of Ording's acquisitions of meadow come first (nos 69–70). Nicholas bought out his brother's rights in the tenement of their uncle Wade son of Ording (no. 66) in a charter which establishes that Gilbert was a smith. Then come fourteen charters in which Nicholas buys land in Kedington (nos 71–84) and two in Sturmer (nos 100–1). In these charters he is shown to have spent a total of £10 10s 8d. There is nothing to show where the money came from, whether the profits of agriculture in a period of generally rising prices, or from some other trade of which the profits were being invested in land. Nor is it possible to say how much was bought, as the land in question is frequently described simply as a 'piece'. The price paid for arable was usually a little over one mark per acre. Eventually Richard, Nicholas's son, gave the land to St Bartholomew's in surprisingly brief terms (no. 89), quitclaims were obtained from Richard's sisters and their husbands (nos 87-8), and from the lord of the holding (nos 85–6). The lord also granted free access (no. 90). There is no sign of payment to Richard, but the priory parted with £4 to each of the sisters and £1 10s for the lord. The date of the transactions has to be before the death of the abbot of Westminster mentioned in the final quitclaims. The Kedington land, which must have been fairly valuable by St Bartholomew's standards, is not mentioned in the *Taxatio* of 1291, nor does it appear in 1382 (no. 129). There is in fact no evidence that the priory actually benefited from the gift.

Many charters do not fall into groups. Some are single deeds of gift to the priory (e.g. nos 3, 4, 63). Others are accompanied by a confirmation or quitclaim from a relative or some other person connected with the land (e.g. nos 29–30). Yet others are not made out to the priory at all. Apart from those which are title deeds for possessions that eventually came to the priory, there is a

[36] See p. 17.

residue of deeds relating to lands that were never given to St Bartholomew's as far as we know. They include a charter of Countess Amice to a servant of hers (no. 5), and a sale of a large tenement in Sudbury in 1318 (no. 41). Most of them relate to Sudbury, but Kedington (nos 67–8) and Melford (nos 93, 98) are also represented. The best explanation for their presence in the priory's archive is that they were deposited there for safekeeping by the owners; the use of religious houses as safe deposits is well known, and in this case the trust has proved very well founded. Some of the depositors were also involved in transactions with the priory (e.g. Alexander son of Richard, no. 39, or Nicholas of Colchester, no. 6), but reasons for the deposit of such documents as Joan Lytil's power of attorney to her father as the executor of her husband's will (no. 57) can only be guessed.

A certain amount can be deduced from the charters about the circumstances under which they were produced. Though a number of deeds have place-dates as well as time-dates only one mentions an occasion, no. 23, the 'full chapter of Sudbury', most likely the ruridecanal synod, before which the prior promised to observe the terms of a charitable donation, and whose members probably witnessed the deed. They included the town reeve. Some deeds may have been witnessed at meetings of a town court, others at informal gatherings.[37] Sometimes the mayor or bailiff of Sudbury is found witnessing with local landowners as well as townsmen (nos 13, 92). On one occasion two separate transactions have identical witness lists (nos 13–14), and once remarkably similar ones (nos 16–17). The people need not all have been present on two occasions: witnesses might perhaps be reinvoked without being reconvened. A group of witnesses occurs frequently in documents relating to the Kedington area, but not in Sudbury deeds: such are, for instance, the various Curpeils and Merilds, Godfrey de Fonte and Robert Palmar. They seem to inhabit a different local circuit of transactions from the Sudbury men.

On a few occasions documents were cut up and reused as the seal tags of charters. No. 38 is particularly revealing: a strip from a charter to St Bartholomew's and Brother Nicholas of Ware, the prior, was used to secure the seal of another document to Prior Nicholas. The piece cannibalized is shown to have been a draft by an interlineation. If drafts of other charters to the priory were available when a document was being drawn up it is a reasonable inference that the priory, and in fact Prior Nicholas himself, was responsible for both drafting charters and having them written. Another possible instance is provided by no. 59, where the seal tag is a reused charter of John son of Benedict, who also occurs as the donor of no. 2. The seal tag document here may have been a faulty version, as it omits the usual 'sancte' from the phrase 'sancte matris ecclesie'. It would not be surprising if the priory, presumably a small centre of literacy and clerical skills, drew up and made charters for itself. This would supply the context for the notes on some charters that they, or what they grant, were 'acquired' by a particular prior or monk – *de perquisitione J. de Wenlac* (no. 32), or *carta Johannis de Rikemeresworth monachi* (no. 22), for instance. The priory might have extended its services, drawing up charters for others. No 84, a late thirteenth-century sale to Nicholas Ording of land in Kedington, incorporates as its seal tag a draft charter almost certainly in favour of Stoke by

---

[37] See below, pp. 15–16.

Clare priory. It seems more likely that the priory would have its own draft charters than that Nicholas Ording would, and so the priory might have had a hand in making the document for a transaction in a nearby village. But another possibility is that a professional scribe reused some of his old waste parchment as seal tags.

As one might hope with a group of original charters, there are many seals.[38] There are fine impressions of the seals of the abbot and convent of Westminster (no. 131) and of Norwich cathedral priory (no. 45). St Bartholomew's own seal survives in a single impression (no. 37). There is Simon of Sudbury's seal before he became a bishop (no. 47), depicting a curious ape-like figure presumably representing a talbot, a medieval hunting dog, which was on the family arms.[39] But the great majority are the seals of very minor local people, including many women. The standard of workmanship of the matrices is not very high (no. 88 is particularly crude), and designs are simple. Radiating star-like lines are a common device, as is a fleur-de-lys. A bird is the commonest representational design. There are three heraldic seals for those of higher social pretentions – two local gentry families (Goldingham, no. 65, and Clopton, no. 90) and a citizen of Westminster (no. 56). Gilbert Mauduit's seal may have incorporated an antique cameo (no. 3). Most of the women's seals are vesica (almond) shaped, though there are exceptions (e.g. no. 20). A few men also have vesica-shaped seals; nos 33 and 34 are unusual in that the man's seal is a vesica and the woman's round. Jordan Merild changed his seal at some stage (cf. nos 79, 84); nos 34 and 35 show that Emma, daughter of Nicholas Ording, changed her seal in widowhood.

The method of sealing is on a tag threaded through a fold in the foot of the document and held together by the wax of the seal impression, except for the correspondence in the Thorpe Morieux tithe case (nos 105–119) where the seal is on a tongue cut parallel to the foot of the document, often with a surviving second strip to tie the letter up with. In a couple of instances a piece of string has survived tied to the tag where no seal remains (nos 29, 30); these may have been added to provide extra key for the wax. The wad of fibrous material that surrounds the seal of no. 10 may be the remains of a method of protecting the seal, in place of the more normal seal bag.

The priory's archive was kept in a group in the Muniment Room at Westminster abbey in the time of Rev. Richard Widmore, Librarian to the Dean and Chapter 1733–64, who drew up an 'Account of the Records' in 1741,[40] and they have been there ever since. They were taken out of their old bundles and given their present numbers by Dr E.J.L. Scott, Keeper of the Muniments 1893–1918, and are in no classified order. It seems certain that the charters must have been at Westminster since the time St Bartholomew's ceased to be a monastic establishment and the property was leased, from 1536, if not before.

There are three distinct sets of endorsements: brief descriptions of the contents of the document, which are often contemporary; a series of Roman numerals, like press-marks, separate from the first series and probably dating from the late thirteenth or early fourteenth century (and thus contemporary with many of the

---

[38] See index.
[39] Azure a talbot sejant within a bordure engrailed argent: see Sperling, 106–7.
[40] WAM Widmore's Catalogue, 53.

documents); and a third series of place-names, apparently later fourteenth- or early fifteenth-century. The numerals are tantalising as they hint at an archive arrangement, yet when all those charters bearing the same number are assembled there is no principle of organisation. Some numbers cover only one surviving document (e.g. x–xii, nos 92, 94, 98), but nos i and ii each cover more than a dozen, and they include all dates from the twelfth to the late thirteenth century, several places besides Sudbury, more beneficiaries than just the priory, and various types of document. Charters from one donor are split between groups: Osbert son of Richard's deeds are endorsed i, ii, iii and iv, for example, and nos 24 and 25, related quitclaims, are assigned different numbers. Documents which may merely have been deposited are also included in the numeration (e.g. no. 5). If the numbers represent some method of storage, the archive was not arranged in accordance with it. There is so little regularity that the existence of groups with only one surviving document does not prove that there have been large losses. The place-name endorsements, mostly Sudbury, Kedington and Melford, use 'Sudbury' to refer to the town, not the priory, as nowhere other than Sudbury is so endorsed. They therefore represent an attempt to organise the priory's archive rather than to keep it separate from other Westminster documents, and might just imply that they were made when the documents were at St Bartholomew's, though the evidence is rather slim. The inventory's endorsement, 'Inventory of the cell of Sudbury', was presumably made at Westminster.

## Sudbury

The charters provide the fullest source for the history of Sudbury in the thirteenth century, for which little else is available. From the fourteenth century and later there are many surviving deeds in various collections, and a large number of account rolls, so no attempt is made here at a history of the later medieval town. But it is worth bringing together what the charters reveal.

For nearly the whole medieval period Sudbury was a seignorial borough: its lords were among the most powerful aristocrats in the country. In 1066 it was held, as Domesday Book says, by 'Earl Morcar's mother', that is to say Aelfgifu, widow of Aelfgar earl of Mercia and mother of Edwin of Northumbria and Morcar of Mercia. In 1086, however, the town came directly under the king.[41] It later came into the possession of the powerful Norman baron Robert fitz Hamo, and Henry I gave it along with many of Robert's other lands to his own illegitimate son Robert, earl of Gloucester. From Earl Robert it passed to his son Earl William, and to William's daughter Amice, countess of Gloucester, as her marriage portion on her marriage to Richard, earl of Clare. In 1198 the couple were separated on grounds of consanguinity, and Countess Amice possessed Sudbury until her death in 1223.[42] It then reverted to the Clare earls of Gloucester, continuing as a demesne manor until the death of the last Clare earl in 1314. The sister of the last earl, Elizabeth de Burgh, Lady of Clare, held it next, and was succeeded by her granddaughter, another Elizabeth, who married

---

[41] DB, fo 286b.
[42] *CRR* i, 186.

Lionel, duke of Clarence. Thence it passed with their daughter Philippa to Edmund Mortimer, earl of March, and down the Yorkist line to be reunited with the crown by Edward IV. It was incorporated into the duchy of Lancaster estates in 1558.[43]

Sudbury counted as a detached part of the hundred of Thingoe – the rest of the hundred was the town of Bury St Edmunds and vicinity, but in the later twelfth century Sudbury did no suit to the hundred, answering only to the king's itinerant justices.[44] Though technically part of the eight-and-a-half hundreds, the liberty of Bury St Edmunds abbey, the abbot's jurisdiction over the town was minimal. There is a stream of litigation from Sudbury on the Curia Regis Rolls and agreements among the final concords to show that it was indeed the king's justices who took cognizance of the town's disputes, even between the lord of the town and the townsmen. An assize was held in 1200 to determine whether Countess Amice and her servants unjustly disseised a man of his free tenement in Sudbury: she admitted it, and was in mercy.[45] On only one occasion, in 1208, are the abbot's bailiffs mentioned, and then not so as to imply that they had any jurisdiction in Sudbury.[46] The only sign of the abbot's authority is the 'general aid of the abbot', a financial levy which he was entitled to raise 'on the whole abbey' (*per totam abatiam*), meaning on the land of the eight-and-a-half hundreds of west Suffolk, including Sudbury (nos 10, 93). In the twelfth century Sudbury was free of the shire court's jurisdiction and from geld dues as well as from the hundred, as we learn from a charter of Henry II. Robert fitz Hamo had granted the manor of Cornard to the nunnery of Malling in Kent, and Henry II ordered that the manor continue to have the same privileges as the town.[47]

In the fourteenth century a good deal is known about the town because of the survival from 1332 onwards of the lord's chamberlain's accounts, covering Sudbury.[48] The lords had a twice-yearly court leet presided over by their bailiffs to try offences less than felony; there was a portmote, the town court, which met perhaps as often as every week, over which the bailiffs also presided. But there are signs in the thirteenth century that Sudbury had some form of communal organisation and a body of customary law of its own. As early as 1217 Countess Amice when founding the hospital of St Sepulchre bound herself not to place anyone there 'without the consent and common counsel of the good men of Sudbury'.[49] Some organ must have existed to express this consent, and it must have been known who the *probi homines* were.

The witness lists of some charters look as though they might represent meetings of such a body, though of course one can never be sure. Where the bailiff, reeve or mayor heads a list of townsmen it is tempting to suppose that the transaction passed in front of a court which they attended. Such are nos 4, 11,

---

43 Sperling, 44–5.

44 DB, fo 286b; *Kal Sam*, 24.

45 *Rot Cur Reg* ii, 180.

46 *CRR* v, 216.

47 *Cal Ch R* v, 58 nos 13, 14.

48 PRO Duchy of Lancaster Ministers Accounts bundle 1006 nos 9–28; Sudbury also appears in accounts of the bailiff of the honour, bundles 1109–14. See Sperling, 19–23. W.O. Ault, *Court Rolls of the Abbey of Ramsey and the Honour of Clare*, New Haven 1928, contains nothing relevant.

49 *Sine consensu et communi consilio proborum hominum de Suberia, Stoke by Clare* no. 63.

15, and 21–2 from the early and mid-thirteenth century; the recurrence of certain names lends more colour to the suggestion. In no. 20 such a group witnesses quite an important agreement, about which there had been litigation on a royal writ. But no. 31's witness list contains men from the surrounding villages as well as townsmen, even though it was given at Sudbury and deals with land there. In no. 92 a similar group of townsmen and others, headed by the mayor of Sudbury, witness a deed dealing with land in Melford. Such gatherings, if indeed they were gatherings at all, could be *ad hoc*, as that at the priory on 25 July 1303 presumably was (nos 87–8).

Thirteenth-century Sudbury also had its own body of customary law. A suit in 1242, between Katharine, widow of Roger of Sudbury, and William de Liketon turned on whether custom entitled a widow to keep all her dowry for life, whether there were heirs or not, or to have half the messuage of which her husband died seised. An inquest was ordered, but we do not know the result.[50]

The following table shows the dates where known and a suggested order for all the reeves, bailiffs and mayors occurring in the St Bartholomew's charters and the thirteenth-century public records:

Ralph de Mullent *prepositus* 1189–90 (no. 2)
Alexander *prepositus* 1208;[51] d. by 1223[52]
Walter Long *prepositus* d. by 1223[53]
Walter *prepositus* 1236;[54] before 1244 (no. 23)
Michael mayor (no. 21)
Gilbert son of Aldred *ballivus* (no. 22)
William son of Warin *ballivus* (no. 11)
            mayor (no. 92)
William son of Elias *prepositus* 1282 (no. 31); d. by Oct. 1286 (no. 96)
Hugh Gauge *prepositus* 1286 (no. 96)

Could it be that the mayors represented the townspeople while the bailiffs and reeves represented and were appointed by the lords? If so, the two mayors whose names we know could be concurrent with some of the other office-holders. What do we know about these men? Nothing can be discovered about Ralph de Mullent or Walter Long, but all the others were Sudbury townsmen, some of them clearly leading citizens. Alexander the reeve, whose son, named Bartholomew, had arable land (nos 13–14), may have been the Alexander son of Gilbert who witnessed charters of Countess Amice and Gilbert Mauduit in the company of scions of local knightly families (nos 3, 5) and who occurs as a servant of the countess in 1200.[55] He may perhaps have been the Alexander of Sudbury who sued Reginald of Cornhill on a plea of debt in 1199,[56] and who therefore must have had some kind of business dealings with that prominent

---

50 *CRR* xvii, no. 821.
51 *CRR* v, 216.
52 *Stoke by Clare* no. 64.
53 *Stoke by Clare* no. 64.
54 *Stoke by Clare* no. 492.
55 *Rot Cur Reg* ii, 180.
56 *Rot Cur Reg* i, 226.

Londoner. If these identifications are correct they make the point that, far from being automatically hostile to their feudal lord, prominent townsmen are quite likely to be found in her entourage.

Michael the mayor was probably the son of Walter the reeve (nos 19–20):

```
        Walter          Osbert son of Richard
          |                      |
        Michael    =    Catharine
```

Michael and Catharine came to an agreement with the prioress of Nuneaton concerning the advowson of St Gregory's in 1257–8: to be dealing with such an important item of property implies that they must have been leading citizens.[57] Another such was William son of Warin, who in a fine of 1240–1 agreed to hold a messuage, 43 acres, 10 acres of wood and 21s in appurtenances with meadow and pasture in Sudbury, Middleton, Goldingham, Binsley and Bulmer for one quarter of a knight's fee, 10s and a pair of gilt spurs.[58] He may have been the son of Warin the clerk, a frequent witness earlier in the thirteenth century and perhaps the Warin *scriptor* accused in a lawsuit in 1208.[59] Gilbert son of Aldred and William son of Elias occur quite often as witnesses of Sudbury deeds without their official title. Hugh Gauge came to an agreement with Geoffrey Gauge about property in Sudbury in 1272–3, and was thus clearly a local man.[60]

All the traceable office holders were therefore local men, some of them among the leading citizens. This does not prevent them from being the lords' appointees: rather it shows that the lords worked through the prominent townsmen. It also suggests that there is little significance in the titles reeve, bailiff or even mayor, since much the same people hold the office.

The lords derived economic benefit from the town in various forms. Most information comes from the time of Countess Amice. There was arable demesne, meadow and pasture, so there was a demesne farm.[61] The countess received rent from the messuages in the town: much of the endowment of St Sepulchre's hospital took this form.[62] She also received rent from the 'selds', semi-permanent stalls in the market place: Walter the goldsmith paid 4d for his.[63] She owned mills, which charged a fee for grinding, and which she might keep herself or let at farm.[64] There was a 'toll' (*tholoneum*), which may have been a market due.[65] Many of these sources still provided revenue in the fifteenth century, when the lords had 800 acres of arable plus meadow and wood, two watermills, rent from '62 ancient booths' and tolls in the market place, fairs on St Bartholomew's day and St Gregory's day and various other rents.[66]

---

[57] Rye, *Fines*, 58; see also BL Add. Ch. 47961.
[58] *Essex Fines* i, 140.
[59] *CRR* v, 216; no. 22.
[60] Rye, *Fines*, 114.
[61] *Stoke by Clare* nos 62–3.
[62] *Stoke by Clare* no. 64.
[63] *Stoke by Clare* no. 65.
[64] *Stoke by Clare* no. 63.
[65] *Stoke by Clare* no. 64.
[66] Sperling, 15–16.

Some information can be gleaned from the charters and other sources about the economic activities of the town. Personal names designating a trade were becoming hereditary in the thirteenth century, but can still be used cautiously to reflect the variety of occupations. As expected, the names baker, miller, carpenter, tanner and smith occur, representing the basic trades of any small town.[67] Textile crafts are to be found in the thirteenth century, with two dyers (Giles and Roger, no. 22) and a fuller (Reginald, no. 34), and evidence of tenter-yards where the cloth was stretched (no. 36): a tenterer occurs in 1305–6.[68] There was a parchment-maker and no less than three painters occur.[69] The making of gloves at Sudbury is evidenced from the early thirteenth century.[70] Philip the merchant occurs in the late thirteenth century (no. 33). Osbert 'the rich' (no. 18) suggests that some people might grow prosperous in Sudbury, and luxury trades are represented by a vintner (no. 9) and a goldsmith (no. 7). Moneyers, such as Wulfric, required some capital; a moneyer was still to be found in the town in 1203.[71]

Sudbury was obviously a trading centre for the locality, and certainly by the fourteenth century had connections beyond the immediate vicinity. The market place and two annual fairs have already been mentioned. In 1202 the men of Sudbury paid the king 20s to be able without loss or injury to buy and sell coloured cloths as the men of Norwich and Bury St Edmunds did and as they themselves had done in the time of Henry II.[72] Further evidence of the cloth trade, as opposed to manufacture, or even the wool trade, is not provided in these charters. Mr Simon of Sudbury's relatives were important wool merchants,[73] and in 1366 Robert Thebaud was licenced to export wheat from Ipswich.[74] A French merchant named Michael Hangard was living, with his wife and children, in Sudbury in the 1330s.[75] In the late thirteenth century there is some evidence of a Jewish community. Moses of Clare was living in Sudbury in 1255.[76] There was enough Jewish business for Sudbury to have its own chirographer in 1269 and 1275.[77] The mysterious *Loqre filius Absalonis* who occurs nearly a century earlier (no. 59) may possibly have been Jewish.

## Editorial method

The documents are arranged in a topographical framework beginning with Sudbury and proceeding to other places in alphabetical order. Within these sections they are in chronological order but with groups referring to the same land or transaction brought together. A 'general' section at the end covers those

[67] See index.
[68] Rye *Fines*, 110.
[69] See index.
[70] Dodwell, *Fines* no. 395.
[71] *CRR* ii, 212.
[72] *PR* 4 John, 115.
[73] VCH *Suffolk* ii, 150.
[74] *Cal Pat R* 1364–7, 224.
[75] *Cal Pat R* 1334–8, 334, 516.
[76] *Cal Pat R* 1247–58, 443; *Cal Pat R* 1266–72, 682.
[77] *Cal Pat R* 1266–72, 382; 1272–81, 127.

relating to many places or none. Those which could date from before 1250 are given in Latin with an English summary; later documents are fully calendared.

Capitalisation has been modernised, with i, j, c and t kept as written if clear in the original, modernised if not. Punctuation has generally been retained as in the original, with the *punctus elevatus* represented by a comma; full stops have sometimes had to be added to end a sentence. Tironian *et* has been rendered as *et*. Spelling oddities have been retained, with a confirmatory footnote to reassure the reader in extreme cases. Uncertain extensions and words supplied are given in brackets. Place-names in calendared documents are given in brackets as written when they first occur in the commonest form, and thereafter in their modern form; exceptional forms are given when they occur. Minor place-names are given in the original form. Dating clauses in calendared documents are given in Latin if there is a witness list; otherwise, in exact English translation with the modern equivalent in brackets.

All documents are on parchment and in Latin. Measurements are across the top and down the right side. Indentures are mentioned as such; the vertical dimension given is the maximum. The size given for seals is that of the impression where complete or calculable, where incomplete it is of the lump of wax. The date given for endorsements is not intended to be more than a rough estimate on palaeographical grounds. Post-medieval endorsements, of which there are very few, are not given.

# CHARTERS

# SUDBURY

1. Confirmation by King Henry I of the gift by Wulfric, his moneyer, in return for fraternity and admission as a monk, to St Peter and the monks of Westminster Abbey, of the church of St Bartholomew of Sudbury; they are to hold the church as was determined by the king's court in the presence of his barons; confirmation of future gifts. April 1114–April 1116.

Henricus rex Anglie Herberto episcopo Norwic' et Haymoni dapifero et burgensibus de Suthberi, omnibusque ministris suis et fidelibus, Francis et Anglis de Suthfolk salutem. Sciatis me concessisse deo et Sancto Petro et monachis Westm(onasterii) pro redemptione anime mee ecclesiam sancti Bartholomei de Suthberia, quam Wlfricus monetarius meus ad usum monachorum inibi servientium eis dederat pro fraternitate et monachatu suo quem ibidem susceperat. Unde uolo et firmiter precipio ut bene et quiete et honorifice et libere et absque omni calumpnia et inquietudine cum terris et decimis cum saca et soca et toll et theam et latrone et cum omnibus rebus et consuetudinibus et legibus verum etiam nunc/(fo 79v) melius et plenius et liberius quam ullo antea tempore habuerant, deinceps teneant eam sicut dirationatum fuit in curia mea coram baronibus meis. Iccirco defendo et prohibeo super x. libras forisfacture ne aliquis eis ulla unquam occasione iniuriam seu torturam faciat, neque eos in aliquo aliquando molestare siue disturbare presumat. Et si quis amodo fidelis pro salute anime sue aut in terris aut in decimis uel in elemosinis siue quocumque alio beneficio eis subuenire uoluerit, hec omnimoda beniuolentia et libertate concedo. Testibus R(adulfo) archiepiscopo, R(icardo) episcopo London' R(ogero) episcopo Sar, R(anulfo) Canc(ellario), Nigillo de Alb(ini) et aliis multis apud Westm'.

BL, Faustina A iii, fo 79r–v.
Pd: *Mon Ang* iii, 459 no. 1; RRAN no. 1178 (abstract); Hodson, 'St Bartholomew's', 18–19 (translation).
Date: Archbishop Ralph elected; Bishop Herbert Losinga of Norwich died in 1119, but the king was in Normandy from April 1116 to 1120
Note: see above, pp. 1–2.


2. Confirmation by John son of Benedict to St Bartholomew's priory, with the consent of his brother William, of a small piece of land, nearly 1½ acres, between *Hiopemere* and the earl's grove, for 1d annually on St Bartholomew's day. 1189–90.

Notum sit uniuersis sancte matris ecclesie filiis qui has literas uiderint uel audierint. quod ego Iohannes filius Benedicti concessi et hac mea presenti carta confirmaui caritatis intuitu deo et Sancto Bartholomeo de Suberia. et monachis ibidem deo seruientibus consenciente et uolente fratre meo Willelmo quandam porciunculam terre iacentem inter Hiopemere et nemus comitis pro redemptione anime mee et patris et matris mee. et omnium parentum meorum. que continet acram et fere dimidiam in perpetuam elemosinam libere et quiete tenendam absque omni calumnia reddendo annuatim unum denarium pro omni seruicio die Sancti Bartholomei. et pro consilio et manutenencia fratrum predicti loci. et hoc factum est primo anno regni Ricardi regis. Radulfo de Mullent existente preposito. et Roberto de Clara. et Martino monachis tunc temporis ibi deo seruientibus. His testibus, Willelmo de Goldinggeham. Nicholao Carbonel. Gileberto de Middeltunia. Roberto clerico de Middeltunia. et Willelmo filio Benedicti. et Roberto de Munteburgh. Nicholao de Braia.

WAM 20759, 20.8 × 9.9 cm. Slits for seal tag.
Endorsed: Johannes filius Benedicti. Suthbyr' (c.1300) j[a]
Date: Richard I was crowned on 3 September 1189. A John son of Benedict held half a carucate in Timworth (*Kal Sam*, 7).

3. Grant in pure and perpetual alms from Gilbert Mauduit to St Bartholomew's priory of a yearly rent of 12d due from Warin the clerk of Sudbury for two acres of meadow at *Dagfen*. Early thirteenth century, possibly before 1223.

Omnibus ad quos presens scriptum peruenerit Gilebertus Mauduit salutem. Nouerit uniuersitas uestra me concessisse et dedisse pro amore dei et salute anime mee et antecessorum et successorum meorum deo et monastario Sancti Bartolomei extra Suberiam constructo et monachis ibi deo seruientibus in puram et perpetuam elemosinam annuum reditum duodecim denariorum illorum scilicet. quos Warinus clericus de Suberia mihi facere debuit pro duabus acris prati aput Dagfen. quas (dedi) eidem Warino et heredibus suis pro homagio et seruicio suo mihi prefacto. Habendas et tenendas iure hereditario per annuum seruicium duodecim denariorum pro omni seruicio et consuetudine et exaccione ad me et ad heredes meos pertinente. Volo igitur et firmiter statuo ut predicti monachi habeant inperpetuum predictum reddictum ita libere et quiete integre bene et pacifice quod nec ego nec aliquis heredum meorum possit a predictis monachis vel a predicto Warino vel heredibus suis pro predicto prato quacumque occasione aliqu(id) aliud seruicium exigere. Ego etiam et heredes mei warantizabimus prefatis monachis predictum redditum contra omnes homines et omnes feminas. Igitur ut hec mea concessio stabilis et firma permaneat, eam presenti scripto et sigilli mei posicione corroboraui. Hiis Testibus. Willelmo Carbonel. Johanne de Goldiggeham. Thoma Carbonel. Ricardo de Bellocampo. Ricardo de Suberia clerico. Alexandro filio Gileberti. Ricardo et Adam filiis eius. Matheo filio Ricardi. Waltero filio Gileberti de Mideltun'. Willelmo filio Roberti. Ricardo filio Beatricis. Alano filio eius. Willelmo Le Bret'.

WAM 20761, 25.7 × 11.5 cm.
Seal on tag: vesica, white wax varnished brown, 3.5 × 3 cm; a winged figure facing right. Possibly antique cameo. +S........MAVDVT
Endorsed: C(arta) Gileberti Mauduth. de xii d. redditus pro ij acris prati in Dagefen (c.1300) j[a]
Date: Alexander son of Gilbert occurs as a servant of Countess Amice in 1200 (*CRR* i, 186); if he was Alexander the reeve of Sudbury, he was dead by 1223 (*Stoke by Clare*, no. 64). Gilbert Mauduit held one knight's fee of the honour of Peverel of London, 1211–12 (*Red Bk* ii, 591). William and Thomas Carbonel occur in a charter

of c.1206–11 (*Kal Sam*, no. 100). John of Goldingham occurs between 1204 (*PR 6 John*, 32) and 1224 (*CRR* xi, no. 2392). Warin the clerk occurs 1217–23 (*Stoke by Clare* no. 64), and may be the Warin *scriptor* who occurs in 1208 (*CRR* v, 216).

4. Grant in free alms from John son of Thomas the parson of St Gregory at Sudbury to St Bartholomew's priory of one acre and one rood of land by the road called *the Melnewei*, in return for 25s. Early thirteenth century.

Sciant presentes et futuri quod ego Johannes filius Thome persone Sancti Gregorii de Suberia dedi. et concessi. et hac presenti carta mea confirmaui deo. et ecclesie Sancti Bartholomei de Suberia et monachis ibidem deo seruientibus unam acram terre et unam rodam de tenemento Suberie que iacent iuxta uiam que uocatur the Melnewei, in puram et perpetuam elemosinam cum omnibus pertinentiis suis liberas. et quietas ab omni exactione. et consuetudine. et seruitio seculari. Pro hac autem donatione. et confirmatione, dederunt mihi predicti monachi viginti et quinque solidos. Hanc autem donationem, ego et heredes mei predictis monachis contra omnes homines et omnes feminas warantizare debemus. Et ut hec mea donatio stabilis. et rata permaneat, eam sigilli mei testimonio roboraui. Hiis testibus. Waltero preposito Suber(i)e. Osberto filio Ricardi. Matheo filio Ricardi. Warino clerico. Willelmo de Venella. et multis aliis.

> WAM 20767, 20.3 × 9.1 cm. Slits for seal tag.
> Endorsed: Johannes filius Thome persone Suthbyr' (c.1300)
> Date: For Walter the reeve, see above, pp. 16–17. For Warin the clerk see no. 3n, for Osbert son of Richard and Matthew son of Richard see no. 5. William de Venella occurs in 1217–23 and 1236 (*Stoke by Clare* nos 64, 492).
> Note: the grammar makes it clear that Thomas was the parson of St Gregory's; he is otherwise unknown.

5. Grant from Amice countess of Clare, daughter of William earl of Gloucester to Abraham son of Ralph of Thaxted of three acres at Holgate in her fee of Sudbury by her wood called Kingswood (*Kinbesuude*) in fee and heredity at a yearly rent of 12d. 1198–1223.

Sciant presentes et futuri quod ego Amicia Comitissa de Clara filia Willelmi Comitis Gloucestrie dedi et concessi et hac presenti carta mea confirmaui Abrae filio Rad(ulfi) de Taxtede pro humagio et seruicio suo tres acras terre arabiles que lancent de terra que fuit Stephani de Holgate usque ad siluam meam que uocatur Kinkesuude iuxta sepem meam que tendit uersus Holgat' in feudo meo de Suberia tenendas et habendas de me et heredibus meis illi et heredibus suis libere et quiete in feudo et hereditate reddendo inde annuatim mihi et heredibus meis duodecim denarios ad duos terminos. scilicet ad pascha sex denarios et ad festum Sancti Michaelis sex denarios pro omnibus seruiciis et exigenciis et consuetudinibus et ego et heredes mei warantizabimus predictam terram predicto Abrae et heredibus suis per prenominatum seruicium contra omnes homines et omnes feminas. Hiis Testibus. Philippo de Hardres. Alexandro filio Giliberti de Suberia. Ricardo clerico filio Johannis. Matheo filio Ricardi. Willelmo filio Rogeri. Willelmo filio Hugonis. Laurentio de Hardres. Rad(ulfo) filio

<br>

Freder(ic)i. Osberto filio Ricardi. Roberto arbalistario. Philippo Cauuel. et multis aliis.

WAM 20773, 12.2 × 9.1 cm. Slits for seal tag.
Endorsed: Amicie Comitisse de Clara. ij$^a$ (13th cent.)
Date: Countess Amice (see above, p. 14). Abraham, servant of the countess, occurs in *Stoke by Clare*, nos 62–3. For Alexander son of Gilbert see no. 3n.

6. Grant from Nicholas son of Thomas of Colchester with the assent of Petronilla his wife, daughter and heiress of William de Venella of Sudbury, to Robert of Sturmer, chaplain of Stambourne (Essex), his grantees, legatees and assigns, of one and a half acres of arable land in the fields of Sudbury abutting on land of St Bartholomew's towards the earl of Gloucester's wood, in return for 36s 8d, and an annual rent of 5d. Mid-thirteenth century.

Sciant presentes et futuri quod ego Nicholaus filius Thome de Colecestria assensu et uoluntate Petronille uxoris mee que fuit filia et heres Willelmi de Uenella de Suberia. dedi concessi et hac presenti carta mea confirmaui. Roberto de Sturemere capellano de Stanburne quandam particulam terre arabilis continentem unam acram et dimidiam iacentem in campis de Suberia videlicet inter terram Willelmi filii Alexandri et terram Johannis Iay. et abutat unum capud super terram monachorum Sancti Bartholomei et aliud capud super terram eorumdem monachorum uersus boscum domini comitis Gloucestr(ie) habendam et tenendam de me et heredibus meis iure perpetuo ipsi Roberto. uel cuicumque illam dare. legare. uel assignare uoluerit reddendo inde annuatim quinque denarios ad duos terminos michi et heredibus meis. scilicet ad Pascha duos denarios et obolum. et ad festum Sancti Michaelis duos denarios et obolum pro omnibus seruiciis. et demandis. et exaccionibus. Pro hac autem donacione. concessione et presentis carte mee confirmacione dedit michi predictus Robertus triginta et sex solidos legalium sterlingorum et octo denarios in gersumam. Et ego predictus Nicholaus et heredes mei warantizabimus predictam terram cum omnibus pertinenciis suis iamdicto Roberto uel cuicumque illam dare. legare. uel assignare uoluerit per predictum seruicium contra omnes homines et feminas in perpetuum. Et eundem Robertum a sequela curie Suberie aquietabimus. Et ut hec mea donacio. confirmacio. et presentis carte mee testimonium robur firmitatis futuris temporibus optineat, presenti scripto pro me et heredibus meis duxi apponendum sigillum meum. Hiis testibus Gileberto filio Aldredi. Michaele filio Walteri. Willelmo de Lichetun. Willelmo filio Warini. Ricardo longo. Ricardo filio Mathei. Rogero de Cantewell'. Samanno fabro. Galfrido carpentario et multis aliis.

WAM 20779, 27.6 × 8.2 cm.
Seal on tag: round, white wax varnished green, 3.4 cm; six radiating petals. + S' NICH DEESTRATE
On face of fold: Carta Roberti de Sturmer' urtil'(?)
Endorsed: Carta Nicholai de Colecestr' de una acra et dimidia terre arabilis. Redditus per annum v. d. scilicet ad Pascha ii. d. et ob' et ad festum Sancti Michaelis ii. d. et ob' (both mid-13th cent.) i$^a$
Date: William de Venella and Richard son of Matthew were alive in 1236 (*Stoke by Clare*, no. 492). Robert, chaplain of Stambourne, occurs in *Stoke by Clare*, no. 581.

William son of Warin held a messuage and land in Sudbury and adjoining places in 1240–1 (*Essex Fines* i, no. 140). Michael son of Walter occurs in 1256–7 (Rye, *Fines*, 58). William 'de Luketon' occurs in 1242 (*CRR* xvii, no. 821). Note: for Nicholas and his family, see above, p. 10.

7. Grant from Nicholas of Colchester, at the request of Petronilla his wife, heiress of William de Venella of Sudbury, to Prior Gilbert and the convent of St Bartholomew's of two acres of arable land towards the vill of Melford at a yearly rent of 4d, in return for 3 marks to Nicholas and 12d to Petronilla. Mid-thirteenth century.

Sciant presentes et futuri quod ego Nicholaus de Colcestria ad instanciam et peticionem Petronille uxoris mee et heredis Willelmi de Venella de Suberia. dedi. concessi. et hac presenti carta mea confirmaui Gileberto priori ecclesie Sancti Bartholomei extra Suberiam. et monachis ibidem deo seruientibus duas acras terre arabilis cum omnibus pertinenciis suis uersus uillam de Meleford. illas uidelicet que abutant unum capud super terram dictorum monachorum et aliud capud super chiminum uiride quod tendit uersus molendinum de Holegate. Habendas et tenendas de me et heredibus meis in perpetuum ipsis et successoribus eorum. Reddendo inde singulis annis quatuor denarios ad duos terminos scilicet ad Pascha duos denarios. et ad festum Sancti Michaelis, duos denarios pro omnibus seruiciis. et exaccionibus consuetudinibus et demandis. et cuiuscumque curie sequelis. Pro hac autem concessione. donatione et presentis carte mee confirmatione dederunt michi predicti prior et monachi tres marcas argenti in gersumam et Petronille uxori mee duodecim denarios ad auamentum presentis cognicionis. Et ego dictus Nicholaus et heredes mei warantizabimus duas predictas acras terre cum suis pertinenciis dictis priori et monachis et successoribus eorum per predictum seruicium contra omnes gentes in perpetuum. Ut autem hec mea concessio et donatio et presentis cartee mee confirmatio futuris temporibus robur firmitatis optineat, presenti scripto sigillum meum apposui. Hiis testibus. Gileberto filio Aldredi. Michaele filio Walteri. Willelmo de Liketun'. Willelmo filio Warini. Willelmo Uisdeluy. Ricardo Rusello tunc seruiente de Sub(eria). Ricardo filio Mathei. Ricardo Longo. Samanno fabro. Alexandro Paulin Willelmo aurifabro. et multis aliis.

WAM 20785, 29.8 × 11.2 cm.
Seal on tag: originally round, fragment, white wax varnished brown, 3.3 × 2.7 cm. See no. 6.
Endorsed: Carta Nicholai Colcestr' de duabus acris terre arrabil'...(13th cent.) Meleford' viij[a]
Date: as no. 6. For Prior Gilbert, see above, p. 5. One William Visdelu occurs from 1214 and was dead by 1238 (*CRR* vii, 155; xvi, no. 508); for William son of William see below, no. 28.

8. Grant from Nicholas de Estrete of Colchester at the instance of Petronilla his wife, heiress of William de Venella, in return for 2 marks sterling, to John, prior of St Bartholomew's, of 1 acre of land in Sudbury, paying to the lords of the fee 4d annually, 2d at Easter and 2d at Michaelmas, and to Nicholas and his heirs one clove at Easter. Mid-thirteenth century.

Sciant presentes et futuri quod ego Nicholaus de Estrete de Colecestr' ad instanciam et peticionem Petronille uxoris mee et h(eredis) Willelmi de Venella dedi concessi et hac presenti carta mea confirmavi Johanni priori ecclesie Sancti Bartholomei extra Subir' et monachis ibidem deo servientibus unam acram terre ....cum pertinentiis suis de feodo de Subir' scilicet de terra que quondam fuit Willelmi filii Benedicti iacentem iuxta terram........ unde unum capud abuttat super terram Alani Boydin et aliud capud super terram Andree Pisemar'. (Tenendam et) habendam de nobis et de heredibus nostris inperpetuum ipsis et successoribus eorum. Reddendo inde singulis annis dominis feodi qui pro tempore fuerint quatuor denarii ad duos terminos anni videlicet ad Pascha duos denarios et ad festum Sancti Michaelis. duos denarios. et mihi et heredibus meis unum clavum giloforatum ad Pascha. pro omnibus serviciis exactionibus consuetudinibus et demandis et cuiuscumque curie sequelis. Pro hac autem donacione concessione et huius carte mee confirmacione dederunt mihi predicti prior et monachi duas marcas sterlingorum in gersumam. Et ego predictus Nicholaus et heredes mei warentizabimus predictam terram cum omnibus pertinenciis suis predictis priori et (monachis et eorum) successoribus per predictum servicium contra omnes gentes inperpetuum. Ut autem hec mea concessio de........ confirmacio futuris temporibus robur firmitatis optineat presenti scripto sigillum meum (apposui. Hiis testi)bus. Willelmo filio Warini. Gileberto filio Aldredi. Willelmo de Berton'. Waltero filio David... Roberto Wrau. Radulfo filio Yvonis et aliis.

WAM 20851, 21.9 × 14.2 cm.
Seal on tag: round but damaged, white wax, 3.1 × 3.4 cm, surface missing: see no. 6.
Endorsed, Carta Johannis de Rykemeresworth monachi Suthbyr' ij[a] (contemporary)
Date: as no. 6.

9. Grant from Roesia daughter of Nicholas de Estrete in Colchester to Prior Gilbert and the monks of St Bartholomew's priory, in return for 14 marks and a yearly rent of 18d, of 5 acres of the fee of Melford and 2 acres of the fee of Sudbury lying to the north of the wood of the earl of Gloucester called Kingswood (*Gingeswode*), which her grandfather William de Venella bequeathed to her. Mid- or late thirteenth century.

Sciant presentes et futuri quod ego Roesia filia Nicholai de Estrete in Colecestr' in libera potestate mea dedi et concessi et hac presenti carta mea confirmaui fratri Gileberto priori ecclesie Sancti Bartholomei extra Suberiam et monachis in eadem ecclesia deo seruientibus septem acras terre arabilis cum omnibus pertinenciis suis. scilicet quinque de feodo de Meleford et duas de feodo de Suberia quas Willelmus de Uenella auus meus in sana memoria sua michi legauit et concessit. Que scilicet due acre iacent sub bosco domini Comitis Gloucestrie qui dicitur Gingeswode a latere aquilonari inter terras dictorum monachorum in longitudinem et latitudinem. habendas et tenendas de me et heredibus meis uel assignatis meis ipsis et successoribus eorum in perpetuum reddendo annuatim michi et heredibus meis uel capitalibus dominis terre memorate. decem et octo denarios ad duos terminos. scilicet nouem denarios ad Pascha et nouem denarios ad festum Sancti Michaelis pro omni seruicio et exaccione et pro omnibus aliis rebus et demandis. saluo seruicio domini regis quantum ad memoratum tenementum dinoscitur pertinere. Pro hac autem donatione et concessione et presentis carte mee confirmatione dederunt michi predicti prior et monachi quatuordecim marcas argenti in gersumam. Et ego predicta Roesia et heredes mei uel mei assignati warantizabimus predictam terram cum omnibus perti-nenciis suis dictis monachis et successoribus eorum per predictum seruicium contra omnes gentes in perpetuum. Debemus insuper ipsos monachos et successores eorum ab omni sequela aquietare et indempnes in hac parte omnino conseruare. Ut autem hec mea donatio et concessio et huius presentis carte mee confirmatio futuris temporibus robur firmitatis optineat presentem cartam sigilli mei munimine duxi corroborandam. Hiis testibus. Willelmo filio Warini. Magistro Waltero fratre eius. Gileberto filio Aeldredi. Ricardo Russel. Ricardo filio Mathei. Ricardo Longo. Ernaldo Pokestreng. Alano filio eius. Warino Hector. Galfrido carpentario. Willelmo de Beitone. Rand(u)l(fo) Page. Samanno fabro. Rogero Standhone. Rogero Wimarch. Radulfo Vinitore. Michaele filio Walteri. Rogero de Sturhull'. Et multis aliis.

> WAM 20789, 20.7 × 11.2 cm.
> Seal on tag, vesica, white wax varnished brown, incomplete, 4 × 2.5 cm; a fleur-de-lys. S' RO...
> Endorsed: Carta de quinque acris terre de feodo de Mileford et de duabus acris terre de feodo de Suburi (late 13th cent.) Sudbur' et Meleford' (14th cent.) v$^a$. Another endorsement erased.
> On front of fold: et octo..
> Date: for the donor's father see nos 6–8.

10. Grant from Roesia daughter of Nicholas de Estrate to Prior Gilbert and the monks of St Bartholomew's priory, in return for 14 marks, of 7 acres lying among the monks' lands near the wood of the earl of Gloucester called *Kingeswode*, bequeathed to her by her grandfather William de Venella, for 18d yearly, payable to Nicholas. Mid- or late thirteenth century.

Sciant presentes et futuri quod ego Roesia filia Nicholai de Estrate dedi. concessi. et hac presenti carta mea confirmaui Gileberto priori ecclesie Sancti Bartholomei extra Suberiam et monachis in eadem ecclesia deo seruientibus septem acras terre arabilis cum omnibus pertinenciis suis que iacent iuxta boscum domini comitis Gloucestr' quod dicitur Kingeswode. et iacent inter terras dictorum monachorum in longitudine et latitudine. quas Willelmus de Venella auus meus michi legauit. pro quatuordecim marcis sterlingorum. habendas et tenendas de me et heredibus meis. bene et in pace. quiete honorifice in perpetuum. Reddendo inde annuatim predicto Nicholao et heredibus suis decem et octo denarios ad duos terminos scilicet ad Pascha nouem denarios. et ad festum Sancti Michaelis nouem denarios pro omni seruicio et exaccione et pro omnibus aliis rebus et demandis. saluo generali auxilio domini abbatis Sancti Edmundi quando ponitur per totam abatiam quod ad tantum tenementum pertinet. Iamdictus uero Nicholaus et heredes sui defendent et warantizabunt totam predictam terram cum suis pertinenciis dictis monachis et successoribus eorum per predictum seruicium contra omnes gentes in perpetuum. Ut autem hec carta futuris temporibus robur firmitatis optineat, predicta Roesia et Nicholaus pater eius presenti scripto signa sua apposuerunt. Hiis testibus. Willelmo filio Warini. Gil(berto filio) Aldredi. Ricardo filio Mathei. Ricardo Russel'. Ricardo Longo. Thoma de Holegat'. Stephano clerico. Rogero Wimark. Galfrido carpentario. Samanno fabro. Arnaldo Pokestrenge. Alano filio eius. et multis aliis.

WAM 20790, 17.4 × 9.1 cm.
Two seals on tags: left, Roesia, fragment 2.3 × 1.7 cm. +S....TH' See no. 9. Wrapped in a wad of fibrous organic material.
Right, probably Nicholas, round, white wax varnished brown, 3.1 cm; six radiating lines. Inscription indecipherable: see no. 6.
Endorsed: Carta Roesie filie Nicholai de Col'...H' carta... cartam valt'... Intra Kynges' iiij$^a$
Date: as no. 9.

11. Quitclaim from Petronilla daughter of William de Venella of Sudbury, widow, to Brother John of Rickmansworth (*Rikemareworze*), monk, and the brothers of St Bartholomew's, in return for five marks, of seven acres of land lying below the wood called *Kingeswode* near the land of the said monks bequeathed by her father to her daughter Roysia. Mid- or late thirteenth century.

Sciant presentes et futuri quod ego Petronilla filia Willelmi de Venella de Subyr'. in legeya potestate et propria viduitate mea. concessi. remisi. et quietum clamaui. pro me et pro heredibus meis. ecclesie Sancti Bartholomei de Subyr'. et fratri Johanni de Rikemareworze monaco et eiusdem loci fratribus. deo seruientibus omne ius. et clamium. quod habui. uel quod aliquo modo habere potui. in septem acris terre arabilis. cum pertinenciis. iacentibus sub bosco quod dicitur Kingeswode. inter terras monacorum Sancti Bartholomei. quas Willelmus pater meus legauit Roysie. filie mee. Ita quod ego dicta Petronilla nec heredes mei. nec aliquis nomine meo. uel heredum meorum. aliquid iuris uel clamii. in predictis septem acris terre cum pertinenciis exigere uel vendicare poterimus in perpetuum. Pro hac autem concessione. remissione. et quieta clamancia pro me et pro heredibus meis. dedit mihi dictus Johannes quinque marcas argenti. In huius rei testimonium, presenti scripto sigillum meum apposui. His testibus. Willelmo filio Warini tunc Balliuo Subyr'. Willelmo Wysdelu. Gilberto filio Adeldr(edi). Waltero filio Dauid. Ricardo filio Mathei. Willelmo de Bertone. Roberto filio suo. Alano Pokestreng. Willelmo filio Alani. Stephano clerico et aliis.

WAM 20842, 16.2 × 9 cm.
Seal on tag, white wax, fragment 2.2 × 1.9 cm.
Endorsed: Carta Petronille filie Willelmi de Venella de septem acris terre in Suthbyr' iij$^a$ (late 13th cent.)
Date: after no. 8.

12. Quitclaim from Alexander and William, sons and heirs of the late Gilbert de Venella of Sudbury to St Bartholomew's priory, in return for one mark, of a messuage in Holgate which they once held of the prior and convent by hereditary right. Late thirteenth century.

Hiis testibus. Ricardo filio Mathei. Waltero filio Michaelis. Alexandro Pawlyn. Gilberto Tok. Alano Boydin. Roberto Ive. Thoma capellano et aliis.

WAM 20776, 22.2 × 5.7 cm.
Two seals: left, Alexander, round, dark wax, 2.7 cm; a pattern of lines. *S' ALEXSAND' F'L GIL';
right, William, round, dark wax, 3 cm; stylized fleur de lys similar to Alexander's. *S' WILL' FIL' GILEB'TI
Endorsed (c.1300) Carta fratris Nicholai de War' de uno mesuagio in Holegate. Suthbyr
Date: Gilbert Tok, Alan Boydin and Robert Ive occur in no. 31, of 1282; Brother Nicholas of Ware may be the 'N. of Ware' who died in 1299–1300 (*Monks*, 29).

13. Grant in free alms from Osbert son of Richard of Sudbury to St Bartholomew's, in return for 6 marks, of five acres at Sudbury near the land which belonged to Bartholomew son of Alexander the reeve under Gilbert de Clare's wood called Kingswood. Early thirteenth century, before 1223.

Sciant presentes et futuri quod ego Hosebertus filius Ricardi de Suberia dedi et concessi et hac presenti carta mea confirmaui. deo et ecclesie Sancti Bartholomei de Suberia et monachis ibidem deo seruientibus pro salute anime mee et pro animabus omnium parentum meorum. quinque acras terre de tenemento Suberie que iacent iuxta terram que fuit Bartholomei filii Alexandri prepositi sub nemore domini Giliberti de Clare quod uocatur Kyngeswde. In puram et perpetuam elemosinam, habendas. liberas et quietas ab omni exaccione et seruicio seculari tam regali quam alio. Pro hac autem concessione et donatione mea dederunt michi predicti monachi Sancti Bartholomei sex marcas argenti et ego et heredes mei warantizabimus prenominatam terram predictis monachis contra omnes homines et contra omnes feminas. Et ut hec mea donatio stabilis et rata permaneat, eam sigilli mei testimonio corroboraui. Hiis testibus. Iacobo de Vaubadon. Ricardo de Middelt'. Alexandro preposito de Suberia. Matheo filio Ricardi. Warino clerico. Waltero Longo. Willelmo de Venella. et multis aliis.

WAM 20792, 19.1 × 8.5 cm.
Seal on tag: round, white wax varnished red, fragment, 3.0 × 3.7 cm; a plant of four leaves. ...GILL' OSBERTI FIL' RICARD..
Endorsed: Osberti filii Ricardi de v. acris iuxta Kingeswode. Suthbyr' (late 13th cent.) Sudburye (15th cent.)
Date: Alexander the reeve was dead by 1223 (*Stoke by Clare* no. 64); James de Valbadun occurs between 1202 and 1220 (*Essex Fines*, 27; *CRR* ix, 226). For other witnesses see nos 3–6.

14. Grant from Osbert son of Richard of Sudbury to St Bartholomew's priory of five acres lying near the grove of Gilbert earl of Clare called Kingswood and of a small piece of land near the field of Guy of Melford, in return for 6½ marks. Early thirteenth century, before 1223.

Sciant presentes et futuri quod ego Osebertus filius Ricardi de Suberia dedi. et concessi. et hac presenti carta mea confirmaui. deo et ecclesie Sancti Bartholomei de Suberia. et monachis ibidem deo seruientibus pro salute anime

31

mee. et pro animabus omnium parentum meorum. quinque acras terre de tenemento Suberie que iacent iuxta terram que fuit Bartholomei filii Alexandri prepositi sub nemore domini Gileberti Comitis de Clara quod uocatur Kingeswde. in puram et perpetuam elemosinam. habendas et tenendas. liberas et quietas ab omni exactione et seruitio seculari. Dedi etiam predicto loco. quandam particulam terre que iacet iuxta campum Widonis de Meleford. Hanc autem terram separat quedam fossa a predicto campo. Pro hac autem concessione. et donatione mea, dederunt mihi predicti monachi Sancti Bartholomei sex marcas argenti et dimidiam. Et ego et heredes mei warantizabimus prenominatam terram predictis monachis contra omnes homines. et contra omnes feminas. Et ut mea donatio stabilis. et rata permaneat, eam sigilli mei testimonio corroboraui. Hiis testibus. Iacobo de Vabadun. Ricardo de Mideltun. Alexandro preposito de Suberi. Matheo filio Ricardi. Warino clerico. Waltero longo. Willelmo de Venella. et multis aliis.

> WAM 20766, 25.2 × 8.4 cm.
> Seal on tag: round, white wax varnished red, 3.5 cm; a plant of four leaves.
> +SIGILL OSBERTI FIL RICARDI
> Endorsed: (Carta) Osberti filii Ricardi de v. acris terre sub Kynguswode (c.1300) iij$^a$
> Date: as no. 13.

15. Grant from Osbert son of Richard of Sudbury to St Bartholomew's of one acre of meadow near its meadow of Lolham in Sudbury in return for 3s. Early thirteenth century, before 1223.

Sciant presentes et futuri quod ego Osebertus filius Ricardi de Subiria dedi et concessi et hac presenti carta mea confirmaui ecclesie Sancti Bartholomei de Subiria et monachis ibidem deo seruientibus unam acram prati que iacet iuxta pratum illorum in Loleholme in puram et perpetuam elemosinam liberam et quietam ab omni exactione et seruicio seculari. Pro hac autem donacione et concessione dederunt mihi predicti monachi tres solidos esterlingorum in gersumam. Et ego et heredes mei predictam acram warantizabimus monachis prenominatis contra omnes homines et omnes feminas. Et ut hec mea donacio stabilis et rata permaneat eam sigilli mei testimonio roboraui. His testibus Alexandro preposito de Subiria. Ricardo de Middelt'. Matheo filio Ricardi. Willelmo de Venella. Waltero le taneur. Warino clerico et multis aliis.

> WAM 20780, 21.4 × 7.4 cm.
> Seal on tag: round, white wax varnished red, 3.5 cm: see no. 14.
> Endorsed: Osberti filii Ricardi de Subir' (mid-13th cent,) de una acra prati in Lolleholm (late 13th cent.) ij$^a$ (date uncertain)
> Date: as no. 13.

16. Grant from Osbert son of Richard of Sudbury to St Bartholomew's of the service due from Robert de Bremdon for the meadow between Holgate and Melford which belonged to Richard Morcoc. Early thirteenth century, before 1223.

Sciant presentes et futuri quod ego Osebertus filius Ricardi de Suberi dedi et concessi et hac presenti carta mea confirmaui deo et ecclesie Sancti Bartholomei

Suberie et monachis ibidem deo seruientibus pro salute anime mee et omnium parentum meorum in puram et perpetuam elemosinam totum seruicium quod Robertus de Bremdon' debuit mihi de prato quod fuit Ricardi Morcoc et iacet inter Holegate et Meleford tenendum et habendum de me et de heredibus meis libere et quiete ab omni exaccione et seculari seruicio. Hanc autem donationem meam warantizabimus ego et heredes mei contra omnes homines et omnes feminas. Et ut hec donatio mea stabilis et rata permaneat, eam sigilli mei testimonio roboraui. Hiis testibus. Ricardo de Sipton' Decano Suberie. Willelmo capellano Omnium Sanctorum. Willelmo capellano Sancti Gregorii. Ricardo milite filio Johannis. Hugone Talemasche. Rogero le Manaunt. Roberto Ridel. Waltero Longo preposito de Suberi. et multis aliis.

> WAM 20784, 22.1 × 8.4 cm; tag for seal.
> Endorsement: Osberti filii Ricardi (13th cent.) ii[a]
> Date: Roger le Manant and Walter Long were dead by 1223 (*Stoke by Clare*, no. 64); Richard son of John occurs in 1200 and 1225–6 (*CRR* i, 359; *Essex Fines* i, 71).

17. Grant from Osbert son of Richard of Sudbury to St Bartholomew's priory of three acres lying by the earl's grove called Kingswood (*Kingeswde*) and the monks' land. Early thirteenth century, before 1223.

Sciant presentes et futuri quod ego Hosebertus filius Ricardi de Suberi dedi et concessi et hac presenti carta mea confirmaui deo et ecclesie Sancti Bartolomei Suberie et monachis ibidem deo seruientibus pro salute anime mee et omnium parentum meorum in puram et in perpetuam elemosinam tres acras terre que iacent inter nemus comitis quod uocatur Kingeswd' et fossam Widonis de Meleford. Que etiam terra extendit se in longum iuxta terram predictorum monachorum. Tenendas et habendas de me et de heredibus meis libere et quiete ab omni exaccione et seculari seruicio. Hanc autem donationem meam warantizabimus ego et heredes mei contra omnes homines et omnes feminas. Et ut hec donatio mea stabilis et rata permaneat, eam sigilli mei testimonio roboraui. Hiis testibus. Ricardo de Sipton'. Decano Suberie. Willelmo capellano Omnium Sanctorum. Willelmo capellano Sancti Gregorii.[1] Ricardo milite filio Johannis. Hugone Talemach'. Rogero le Manant. Waltero Longo preposito de Suberi. et multis aliis.

> [1] ms Gregrorii

> WAM 20788, 20.1 (top) 21.4 (bottom) × 8.1 cm; slits for seal tag.
> Endorsed: Osberti filii Ricardi de tribus acris inter Kingeswode et Wythesdic' (late 13th cent.) Sudbury iiij[a]
> Date: as no. 16.

18. Grant from Osbert son of Richard of Sudbury to Alice daughter of Osbert the rich of Sudbury of the service due from Baselia Forstes for a meadow between those of Agnes, widow of William the reeve of the hundred of Babergh, and of St Bartholomew's priory; after Baselia's death Alice, her heirs and assigns shall hold the meadow at a yearly rent of 1d. Early thirteenth century, before 1223.

Sciant presentes et futuri quod ego Osebertus filius Ricardi de Suberi dedi et concessi et hac presenti carta mea confirmaui Alicie filie Oseberti diuitis de Suberi pro humagio et seruicio suo seruicium quod Baselie Forstes debuit mihi pro quodam prato scilicet[1] illo quod iacet iuxta pratum Agnetis relicte Willelmi prepositi del hundred de Baberie ex una parte et iuxta pratum monachorum Sancti Bartholomei de Suberi ex altera parte. ad uitam predicte Baselie. et post discessum Baselie, predicta Aliz et heredes sui uel cui assignare uoluerit tenebit predictum pratum de me et heredibus meis libere et quiete et hereditabiliter reddendo inde annuatim mihi et heredibus meis unum denarium ad festum Sancti Michaelis pro omni seruitio et exactione. Hanc autem donationem et concessionem ego et heredes mei warantizabimus predicti Aliz et heredibus suis contra omnes homines et omnes feminas. Et ut hec donatio mea rata et stabilis permaneat eam sigilli mei roboraui. Hiis testibus. Hugone Thalemasche. Johanne de Hobouile. Rogero le Manant. Ricardo filio Mag(ist)ri. Johanne Ridel. Roberto le Melun. et multis aliis.

[1] ms silicet

WAM 20791, 20.1 × 8.8 cm; slits for seal tag.
Endorsed: jᵃ
Date: as no. 16. John de Hodeboville held a fee of the honour of Peverel of London in Acton (*Red Bk* ii, 478, 591): men of this name occur throughout the thirteenth century.

19. Quitclaim from Michael son of Walter and his wife Katharine daughter of Osbert son of Richard of Sudbury to St Bartholomew's of three acres of land given to the monks by Osbert son of Richard lying between Kingswood and the ditch of Guy of Melford; and grant of the service from a meadow which Richard Morcoc once held of Osbert son of Richard. Early or mid-thirteenth century.

Omnibus Christi fidelibus ad quos presens scriptum peruenerit. Michael filius Walteri. et Katerina filia Oseberti de Subr' uxor sua salutem in domino. Nouerit uniuersitas uestra nos caritatis intuitu concessisse. confirmasse. et quietas clamasse pro nobis. et heredibus nostris in perpetuum deo et ecclesie Sancti Bartholomei Subr' et monachis ibidem deo seruientibus pro salute animarum nostrarum. et omnium parentum nostrorum in puram. liberam. et perpetuam elemosinam. illas tres acras terre arabiles cum pertinenciis. quas Osebertus filius Ricardi eis dedit. et carta sua in puram et perpetuam elemosinam confirmauit. videlicet illas tres acras terre cum pertinenciis iacentes inter boscum quod uocatur Kingeswode. et fossam Widonis de Meleford. et se se extendunt in longum iuxta terram predictorum monachorum. Preterea concessimus et confirmauimus deo et ecclesie predicte Sancti Bartholomei et dictis monachis ibidem existentibus totum seruicium cuiusdam prati quod Ricardus Morcoc aliquando tenuit de predicto Oseberto filio Ricardi cum omni re. iure. et libertate quod in predicto reditu. siue in predicto prato habere potuimus. Tenenda. et habenda in puram. liberam et perpetuam elemosinam inperpetuum absque omni seculari seruicio. Ita tamen quod nos nunquam aliquid iuris. uel clamii in predicta terra cum pertinenciis. uel in predicto redditu. siue in predicto prato exigere. uel uendicare poterimus. Et ut hec nostra concessio. et confirmacio

34

Sudbury

stabilis et rata inperpetuum permaneat sigillorum nostrorum apposicione eam corroborauimus. Hiis testibus. Domino Willelmo de Bridebec. Domino Roberto Ridel. Willelmo de Lauele. Warino clerico. Willelmo de Liketon'. Nigello coco. et multis aliis.

WAM 20843, 16.8×7.5 cm; tags for two seals: left, no seal remaining.
Right: vesica, white wax varnished red, 3.3×2.3 cm, a flowering plant. +S'
K....INE FILIE OSEBERTI
Endorsed: Michael filii Walteri prepositi (mid-13th cent.) vjᵃ (late 13th cent.)
Date: Michael and Katharine occur in 1256–7 (Rye, *Fines*, 58), William de Liketon in 1242 (see no. 6), Robert Ridel in 1236 (*Stoke by Clare*, no. 493), and Warin the clerk in 1217–23 (see no. 3). William de Bridebec was Countess Amice's seneschal before 1223 (*Stoke by Clare*, no. 58).
Note: the grants are those in nos 16 and 17. For Michael son of Walter see above, p. 17.

20. Quitclaim from William le Fatte of Sudbury and Margery his wife to St Bartholomew's priory of a half share in eight acres of arable land of the priory's fee and in a rent of 18d annually from the meadow which belonged to Richard Morcok, to which William and Margery have established a claim by royal writ of dower; renunciation of all claim to dower in lands or possessions granted to the priory by the late Osbert son of Richard of Sudbury, concerning which there was a lawsuit between them and the priory, in return for which they received from Brother Gilbert, the procurator of the priory, and Brothers Alan and John living there as monks, two quarters of corn and one measure of oats. Early thirteenth century.

Omnibus Christi fidelibus presens scriptum inspecturis uel audituris. Willelmus le Fatte de Suberia et Margeria uxor sua salutem in domino. Nouerit uniuersitas uestra nos karitatis intuitu remisisse et quietum clamasse pro nobis et heredibus nostris in perpetuum deo et ecclesie Sancti Bartholomei extra Suberiam totum ius et clamium quod habuimus uel habere potuimus in dimidiam partem octo acrarum terre arabilis cum pertinentiis suis de feodo dicte ecclesie. et dimidiam partem decem et octo denariorum redditus de prato quod fuit Ricardi Morcok que per breue domini regis nomine dotis diracionauimus. Preterea. renunciauimus pro nobis et heredibus nostris in perpetuum omni iuris auxilio ecclesiastici et ciuilis sub fidei sacramento et bonorum uirorum testimonio contra dictam ecclesiam occasione dicte remissionis et clamii. aut donationis seu uendicionis terrarum seu possessionum dicte ecclesie concessarum per bone memorie Osbertum filium Ricardi de Suberia nomine cuius lis inter nos et predictam ecclesiam extitit mota super dote memorata aliquando euenire. Et si contingit quod ego Margeria uiro meo superuixerim, me in uiduitate existente, nunquam occasione clamii prenominati aliquid a predicta ecclesia uel fratribus qui pro tempore illi ecclesie prefuerint exigere potero uel habere. In cuius rei testimonium et signum pacifice compositionis dederunt nobis frater Gil' tunc dicte ecclesie procurator et fratres Alanus et Johannes monachi cum ipso commorantes duo quarteria frumenti et unam summam auene. Nos uero scilicet ego prenominatus Willelmus nomine meo et ego dicta Margeria ipsius Willelmi sponsa similiter nomine meo sponte et non coacta signa nostra in robur perpetue

35

firmitatis presenti scripto decreuimus apponenda. Hiis testibus. Waltero preposito de Suberia. Michaele filio suo. Roberto Ridel clerico. Warino clerico. Gileberto filio Audri. Willelmo de Venella. Alexandro filio eius. Willelmo de Liketun'. Waltero le tanur. Bartholomeo de Liketun'. Alexandro de Storhulle. Symone cementario. Willelmo le Rutur. et multis aliis.

> WAM 20771, 17.2 × 14.2 cm.
> Two seals on tags: left, nearly round, white wax, 3.5 × 3.2 cm; fleur de lys of five leaves, inscription illegible.
> Right, round, white wax, 3.4 cm; a standing bird with outstretched wings, inscription illegible.
> Endorsed: Quiet' clam' Willelmi le Fatte et Margerie uxoris sue ... dimidietate octo acrarum terre arabilis. Sudbur' vij$^a$ (14th cent.)
> Date: for William de Venella see no. 4, for Warin the clerk see no. 3; for Walter the reeve of Sudbury, see above, pp. 16–17. Simon the mason lived next door to St Sepulchre's church, 1217–23 (*Stoke by Clare*, no. 64).

21. Grant from Alexander son of Richard of Sudbury to St Bartholomew's of one acre to the east of St Bartholomew's church, paying 4d annually. Mid-thirteenth century.

Sciant presentes et futuri quod ego Alexander filius Ricardi de Subir' dedi et concessi et hac presenti carta mea confirmaui deo et ecclesie Sancti Bartholomei extra Sutbir' inpuram et liberam et perpetuam elemosinam unam acram terre cum omnibus pertinenciis suis in villa de Sutbir' que iacet ex parte orientali ecclesie Sancti Bartholomei ex utraque parte inter terras monachorum eiusdem loci habendum et tenendum de me et de heredibus meis et meis assingnatis dicte ecclesie Sancti Bartholomei et monachis ibidem deo seruientibus et eorum successorum uel cuicumque illam dare vendere uel assingnare voluerint et eorum heredibus libere quiete honorifice bene et inpace inperpetuum reddendo inde annuatim mihi et heredibus meis quatuor denarios ad duos terminos anni. scilicet ad Pascha duos denarios et ad festum Sancti Michaelis duos denarios pro omnibus seruiciis. consuetudinibus. sectis curie exaccionibus et pro omnibus rebus aliis et ego predictus Alexander et heredes mei et assignati mei warantizabimus. aquietabimus et defendemus predictam terram cum omnibus pertinenciis suis predicte ecclesie Sancti Bartholomei et monachis ibidem deo seruientibus ut puram. liberam et perpetuam elemosinam per predictum seruicium contra omnes homines et feminas in perpetuum. In cuius rei testimonium presenti scripto sigillum meum apposui. Hiis testibus Michaele tunc maior' de Sutbir' Willelmo filio Warini Waltero de Clopton' Gileberto filio Aeldredi Ricardo filo Mathei Johanne Darel Egidio tinctore Willelmo de Liketone Bartholomeo de Liketone Roberto Wrau Willelmo Helkyn Hugone Gaugi Maur(icio) pictore Willelmo Snau et multis aliis

> WAM 20786, 25.9 × 11.6 cm.
> Seal on tag, round, green wax, 3.2 cm; a five-branched tree-like device. + S' ALEX PAVLIN
> Endorsed: Carte Alexandri Paulyn de Sutbyr' (late 13th cent.) ii$^a$
> Date: William son of Warin occurs in 1240–1, Richard son of Matthew in 1236, William de Liketon in 1242 (see no. 6). Walter of Clopton occurs between 1230 and

1258 (*CRR* xiii, no. 2351; *Exc e Rot Fin* ii, 292). For Hugh Gauge see below, no. 27. See also no. 38.

22. Grant from Alexander son of Richard of Sudbury to St Bartholomew's, in return for 16s, of three roods of land in Sudbury for a yearly rent of 6d. Mid-thirteenth century.

Sciant presentes et futuri quod ego Alexander filius Ricardi de Suberia concessi et dedi et hac presenti carta mea confirmaui deo et ecclesie Sancti Bartholomei iuxta Suberyam et monachis ibidem deo seruientibus tres rodas terre cum pertinenciis iacentes inter terram Willelmi filii Warini clerici ex una parte. et terram dictorum monachorum ex altera. Et habutant ad unum caput super foueam de Kyngeswode et aliud super terram dictorum monachorum. Tenendas et habendas de me et de heredibus meis dictis monachis et eorum successoribus libere. quiete. bene. et in pace. iure hereditario finabiliter. Reddendo inde annuatim mihi et heredibus meis sex denarios. scilicet ad Pascha tres denarios et ad festum Sancti Michaelis tres denarios. pro omnibus seruiciis. exigenciis consuetudinibus et pro omnibus rebus. Et ego dictus Alexander et heredes mei warantizabimus predictas tres rodas cum pertinenciis suis dictis monachis et eorum successoribus ibidem deo seruientibus in perpetuum per predictum seruicium contra omnes gentes. Pro hac autem concessione et donacione et huius carte confirmacione dederunt mihi predicti monachi sexdecim solidos esterlingorum in gersumiam. Et ut hec mea concessio et donacio et presentis carte mee confirmacio et warentizacio rata et stabilis in perpetuum permaneat presenti carte mee signum meum apposui. Hiis testibus. Gilberto filio Audre. tunc temporis balliuo de Suberya. Willelmo Uisdelu. Michaele filio Walteri. Willelmo de Liketone. Rogero tinitore Alexandro de Sturhille. Willelmo de uenella. Galfrido capellano. Willelmo filio Audre Et multis aliis.

WAM 20833, 16.6 × 8.9 cm.
Seal on tag, round, light brown wax varnished dark brown, fragment 3.5 × 2.7 cm; an assymmetrical five-pointed star +S' ALEXANd...RDI
Endorsed: Carta Johannis de Rikemeresworth' monachi de tribus rodis terre in Suthbyr iij$^a$ (late 13th cent.)
Date: for William Visdelu see no. 7, for William de Venella no. 4; for Matthew son of Walter and William de Liketon see no. 6. See also no. 38.

23. Grant from Richard son of Alexander of Sudbury to St Bartholomew's Priory of a rent of 2s from Geoffrey Lurt from the fee Geoffrey holds of Richard in Holegate, to provide a lamp before St Bartholomew's altar. Early thirteenth century, before 1244.

Sciant......... filius Alexandri de Subir' concessi et hac presen......... de Subir' et monachis ibidem............. sinam. quos Alexander pater............ lampadem ardentem coram altare Sancti Bartholomei............. Sancti Michaelis per manum Galfridi Lurt et heredum suorum percipiendos de feodo quod dictus Galfridus Lurt tenet de me in Holegate. promisit autem predictus prior Sancti Bartholomei in bona fide in pleno capitulo de Subir' pro se et successoribus suis quod predicti ij. solidos.... a lampade fideliter expenduntur. Hiis testibus.

Magistro Ricardo de Berton.... Subir'. Willelmo vic(ario).... Suberie. Stephano pesone Sancti Gregorii de Subir'. Rob....clerico. Waltero preposito Suberie. Johanne filio Ricardi. Warino clerico et multis aliis.

> WAM 20769, 11.8 × 7.1 cm; damaged by damp.
> Seal on tag: round, white wax, 3.5 cm; a bird facing right, inscription illegible.
> Endorsed: Ricardi filii Alexandri de Subyr'
> De ij.s'. pro lampade. (Both c.1300) v$^a$
> Date: Stephen was rector of St Gregory's in 1236 (*Stoke by Clare*, no. 492) and Adam of Bromholm had succeeded by 1244 (BL Add. Ch. 47959).

24. Quitclaim by Richard son of Pain (*Paganus*) and Aveline his wife to the monks of St Bartholomew's in return for 2s 6d of all their rights in the curtilage formerly held of the said church by Pain the baker at Holgate opposite the monks' meadow. Late thirteenth century.

Hiis testibus. Hugone filio Ade. Roberto Wyth.' Radulfo filio Yuonis. Ricardo pictore. Henrico pargamenario et aliis.

> WAM 20777, 16.2 × 6.2 cm.
> Two seals on tags: left, round, white wax, 3.5 cm; sixteen-pointed radiating design.
> +S' RICARDUS FIL PAGANI
> Right, vesica, white wax, 4.2 × 2.7 cm; design indecipherable. +S AVELINE FELIE RANULFI
> Endorsed: Carta Ricardi filii Pagani de curtilagio in Holegate (c.1300) ij$^a$
> Date: Hugh son of Adam occurs in 1276 and 1286, and was dead by August 1307 (*Aug Friars*, nos 26, 28, 56).

25. Quitclaim from John son of Pain to St Bartholomew's in return for 14d, of a plot of land (*placea*) which Pain his father formerly held of the priory opposite the monks' meadow in Holegate, next to the messuage of Alice Scaterun. Late thirteenth century.

Hiis testibus. Hugone filio Ade. Roberto filio Willelmi de Elmeswell'. Hugone filio Ade de Meleford'. Radulfo filio Yuonis. Ricardo Bodin. Rogero de Laueham'. et multis aliis.

> WAM 20838, 14.5 × 6.2 cm.
> Seal on tag, white wax, fragment 2.5 × 3 cm; S. IOH..
> Endorsed: Quieta clamancia J. filii Pagani de una placia in Holegat'. Suthbyr' (late 13th cent.) j$^a$
> Date: as no. 24.

26. Grant from William son of Warin the clerk of Sudbury to Prior Gilbert and the monks, in return for 30s in *gersuma*, of three roods of arable land next to the monks' land and the wood of the earl of Gloucester, and of half an acre of arable land, for a yearly rent of 2d. Early to mid-thirteenth century.

Sciant presentes et futuri quod ego Willelmus filius Warini clerici de Subiria concessi dedi et hac presenti carta mea confirmaui Gilleberto priori ecclesie

Sancti Bartholomei extra Subiriam et monachis ibidem deo seruientibus tres rodas terre arabilis cum omnibus suis pertinenciis que iacent iuxta terram eorumdem monachorum. et abuttat unum capud super boscum domini comitis Glouern(ie). et aliud capud super terram eorumdem monachorum. et dimidiam acram terre arabilis cum suis pertinenciis que iacet iuxta terram Rogeri Flandrensis et terram Bartholomei de Liketun' uersus aquilonem. Tenendas et habendas de me et de heredibus meis ipsis et successoribus eorum imperpetuum reddendo inde singulis annis duos denarios ad duos anni terminos. scilicet ad Pascha unum denarium. et ad festum Sancti Michaelis unum denarium. pro omnibus seruiciis et demandis et curie sequelis. Pro hac concessione donacione et presentis carte mee confirmacione dederunt michi dictus prior et monachi triginta solidos in gersumam. et ego dictus Willelmus et heredes mei warantizabimus predictas particulas terre cum suis pertinenciis dictis monachis et eorum successoribus contra omnes homines et feminas per predictum seruicium imperpetuum. Ut autem hec mea concessio donacio et huius presentis carte mee confirmacio robur firmitatis futuris temporibus optineat, presenti scripto sigillum meum apposui. Hiis testibus. Gilleberto filio Aldredi. Michaele filio Walteri. Willelmo de Liketun'. Willelmo Visdeluy. Waltero filio David'. Rogero Flemeng'. Rogero clerico. Rogero Standon. Alexandro Leker. et multis aliis.

> WAM 20824, 17.1 × 12.2 cm. Tag for seal.
> Endorsed: Carta Willelmi filii Warini clerici de Subiria de tribus rodis terre et de dimidia acra terre. Redditus per annum ij. d. soluendus jᵃ (c.1300) Sudbur' (15th cent.?)
> Date: the donor occurs in 1240–1, Michael son of Walter in 1256–7, William de Liketon in 1242 (see no. 6). For William Visdelu see no. 7.
> Note: for William son of Warin see above, p. 17.

27. Confirmation from Thomas son of William Warin of Sudbury to Henry, prior and the monks of St Bartholomew's, in return for 4s of silver, of three roods of arable land next to the monks' land, abutting on the earl of Gloucester's wood and on the monks' land; and of half an acre of arable land next to land formerly belonging to Roger Fleming (*Flanrensis*) and Bartholomew *de Lyketon* as contained in the charter of enfeoffment (*carta feoffamenti*) of William, Thomas's father; paying yearly 1d at Easter and 1d at Michaelmas; warranty against all men and women. Late thirteenth century.

Hiis testibus. Domino Johanne de Hodebouil'. Domino Hugone Talemach' militibus. Roberto de Berton'. Hugone Gauge. Gilberto de Acra. Ada Wyth Galfrido filio Th(ome). Gilberto Thoke. et aliis.

> WAM 20855, 18.6 × 15.8 cm. Tag for seal.
> Endorsement: Carta Thome filii Willelmi Warini de Subyr' de tribus rodis terre et dimidiam acram terre (14th cent.) ijᵃ Sudbir' (15th cent.?)
> Date: Hugh Gauge occurs in 1272–3 (Rye, *Fines*, 114) and in 1282 (below, no. 31). One Hugh Talemache died in 1296, but was succeeded by another (*Cal IPM* iii, no. 389); a John de Hodeboville witnessed a deed of 1293–4 and died in 1300 (PRO, Ancient Deed C2450; *Cal IPM* iii, no. 634). Adam Wyth ocurs in 1286 (below, no. 96).
> Note: the charter referred to is no. 26.

28. Grant from William son of William Le Witdelu of Sudbury to Gilbert *de Houesden*, chaplain, his heirs, assigns, grantees and legatees, in return for 3s 6d in *gersuma*, of a yearly rent of 6½d for a piece of land held of the said William and Gilbert by Alexander Cokelin at Holgate, lying between Gilbert's land on either side and abutting at one end on St Bartholomew's land and at the other on the road from Sudbury to Melford (*Mellefordia*), paying yearly one clove (*clavem giloforatum*) at Easter. Warranty against all people. Late thirteenth century, before 1286.

Hiis testibus. Willelmo filio Elys. Hugone Gauge. Thoma de Sturhylle. Willelmo de Hausted. Willelmo Liketon'. Willelmo Persun. Alexandro Cokelin. Thoma clerico. Gilberto Willes. clerico et multis aliis.

> WAM 20837, 19.8 × 12.7 cm. Slits for seal tag. Not endorsed.
> Date: William son of Elias was dead by 1286 (below, no. 96). Thomas of Sturhill occurs in 1299 and 1300 (below, nos 35, 37). For Hugh Gauge see no. 27.

29. Quitclaim from Matilda widow of Ralph Yve of Melford to St Bartholomew's, in return for 12s in cash (*premanibus*), of a piece of meadow in the suburb of Sudbury, lying between the meadow of Agnes widow of the reeve of the hundred of Babergh (*Baberye*) and that of the priory, paying 1d yearly at Michaelmas to the chief lord of the fee, to sustain a lamp before the altar of the Virgin in the priory church. Mid- to late thirteenth century.

Hiis testibus. Willelmo filio Warini. Michaele filio Walteri. Ricardo filio Mathei. Ada Wyd'. Gilberto Toke. Galfrido le Heyward. Willelmo filio Andree. Stephano clerico. et. aliis.

> WAM 20831, 19.2 × 11.9 cm.
> Seal on tag, vesica, brownish wax, 3.9 × 2.5 cm; a cross, the arms divided by diagonal lines. S' MATILDIS... A small piece of string is tied onto the tag.
> Endorsed: Carte fil' Roberti Yve de Mulefeld' ij[a]
> Date: William son of Warin occurs 1240–1 (see no. 6), but Adam Wyth, Geoffrey the hayward and Gilbert Toke in the 1280s (see nos 31, 96). For Michael son of Walter see no. 6.

30. Confirmation by Robert son of Ralph Yve (*Yue*) of Melford of the grant from Matilda his mother to St Bartholomew's of one meadow in the suburb (*suburbium*) of Sudbury lying between that of Agnes widow of the reeve of Babergh hundred (*prepositi Hundredi de Babberewe*) and that of the monks, for the maintenance of a lamp before the Virgin's altar in the priory church, paying yearly at Michaelmas 1d and a clove (*clauum gariofilatum*); warranty against all men and women. Mid- to late thirteenth century.

Hiis testibus. Gileberto filio Aldr(edi). Willelmo filio Warini. Michaele filio Walteri. Ricardo filio Matthei. Ada Wyth. Gileberto Tok. Galfrido Messario. Willelmo filio Andree. Stephano clerico et multis aliis.

> WAM 20821, 15.8 × 11.5 cm; tag for seal, with knot of string attached, perhaps to provide extra key for seal.

Endorsed: De prato in Holgate iij$^a$ (14th cent.)
Date: as no. 29. Robert Ive occurs in no. 31, 1282.


31. Grant from William Pat of Holgate (*Hollegate*) to St Bartholomew's, in return for 20s in cash (*premanibus*), of one acre of his meadow in Sudbury enclosed on all sides by the monks' meadow and ditch, for a yearly rent, payable at Michaelmas, of 2d to William and his heirs; warranty against all people. Given at Sudbury, 7 July 1282.

Hiis testibus. Willelmo filio Elye tunc preposito Subyr'. Willelmo de Lyketon' de Subyr'. Hugone Gauge de eadem. Galfrido filio Thome de Meleford. Roberto Iue. Alano Bodin. Ada Wyth de eadem. Hugone de Grangia de Waudingfeud. Gilberto et Ada filiis suis. Simone Thurgor de Aketon'. Gilberto Thoke de eadem. et aliis. Dat' apud Subyr' die translacionis Beati Thome Martiris. anno regni regis Edwardi decimo.

> WAM 20794, 22 × 13.1 cm.
> Seal on tag, fragment 2.7 × 2.0 cm, originally circular, white wax: see no. 32.
> Endorsed: Carta quondam Willelmi Pat per fratrem Ricardi de Dol inpetrata De una acra prati pro solucione ij.d. Suthbyr (late 13th cent., three different hands) j$^a$


32. Quitclaim from William Pat of Holegate to the prior and convent of St Bartholomew's, in return for 20d in cash (*premanibus*) in *gersuma*, of a yearly rent of 2d due from one acre of meadow in Sudbury lying in the monks' enclosed meadow surrounded by their ditch. Late thirteenth or early fourteenth century.

Hiis testibus Jacobo de Peitune Benedicto de Stansted Galfrido Duniel Nicholao Pod Gileberto de Grangia et multis aliis

> WAM 20879, 25 × 7 cm.
> Seal on tag: round, dark brown wax, 2.3 cm; six radiating petals. *S WILL'I. PAT.
> Endorsed: (14th cent.) De perquisicione J. de Wenlac. W Pathog de Holgate ijd' ij$^a$
> Date: the rent was granted in no. 31. James of Peyton occurs in 1303 (below, nos 87–8); 'J de Wenlac' is possibly John of Wenlock, who occurs as a monk of Westminster from 1296 and was still alive in 1323 (*Monks*, 67).


33. Grant from Roger de Riueshal and Alice his wife to Geoffrey de Riueshal, Emma his wife and John their son and to whomever they may grant, leave, sell or assign it, in return for 20s in *gersuma*, of a piece of meadow in Sudbury called *le Cope*, between the land of the monks of St Bartholomew's and the River Stour flowing towards Holgate mill, for an annual rent of 1d payable at Michaelmas. Warranty against all people. Late thirteenth century.

Hiis testibus. Waltero filio Michaelis. Hugone Gauge. Willelmo filio Elis. Alexandro Paulin. Roberto de Berton'. Ricardo filio Mathei. Roberto Dereman. Philippo mercatore. Roberto Longo. Mauricio filio Gilberti Gilberto de Grangia. et aliis

> WAM 20827, 17.8 × 9.5 cm.

Two seals on tags, dark reddish wax. Left: rounded vesica, 2.6 × 2.2 cm; two fleurs-de-lys top to bottom. * S' ROG'I D' RIVISh'
Right: round, 2.4, a seven-branched candlestick. *S' ALICIE. FIL'. RAD'I
Endorsed: Carta Rogeri de Ryueshal' de una pecia prati que vocatur le Cope Sudbury (14th cent.?) j<sup>a</sup>
Date: see nos 34–5.

34. Grant from Geoffrey de Ryueshale of Sudbury and Emma his wife to Brother Henry of London, prior, and the convent of St Bartholomew's, in return for two marks in cash (*premanibus*), of all their meadow within the prior's enclosed meadow, between the prior's meadow and the river Stour (*Sture*), abutting on the mill pool of Holgate, for an annual rent of 1d at Michaelmas; warranty against all people. Late thirteenth century.

Hiis testibus. Thoma de Sturhyll. Hugone Gauge. Gilberto de Aqua. Reginaldo fullone. Galfrido filio Thome. Roberto Iue. Alano Boydin. Ada de Wythes. Simone Thurgor. Ricardo fratre suo. Hugone de Grangia. Gilberto filio suo. Gilberto Thoke. et aliis.

WAM 20881, 23 × 16.6 cm.
Two seals on tags: left, Geoffrey de Reveshal: round, dark brown wax, 2.9 cm; a six-petalled flower. + S' GAL....D' REVESHA'
Right, Emma de Reveshal: vesica, dark brown wax, 3.6 × 2.4 cm; a fleur-de-lys and its reflection. * S' EMME...GALFR'
Endorsement: Carta Emme de Ryueshale ij<sup>a</sup> (14th cent.)
Date: the meadow is almost certainly that acquired in no. 33; Geoffrey de Riveshall was dead by 1300 (no. 35).

35. Quitclaim from Emma, widow of Geoffrey de Reueshale of Sudbury, to Abbot Walter and the convent of Westminster and Prior Simon and the monks of St Bartholomew's, in return for an unspecified sum of money, of her rights and claims in a piece of meadow called 'Le Cope' in Sudbury, lying between the monks' meadow and the Stour (*Stura*) running towards the mill of Holgate; saving 1d annual rent. Given at Sudbury, 12 March 1300.

Hiis testibus. Roberto de Berton' Galfrido de Netlisted Henrico Schingel. Willelmo de Meudon' Thoma Warin. Thoma de Sturhill'. Waltero de Bellocampo. Willelmo Bere. Petro Stendut. Stephano de Chilton et aliis. Dat' apud Subir' die mercurii proxima post festum Sancti Gregorii pape anno Regni Regis Edwardi filii Regis Henrici vicesimo octavo.

WAM 20816, 19.3 × 12 cm.
Seal on tag, vesica, white wax, 2.5 × 1.8 cm; radiating lines. ...TE DE RE...
Endorsed: Quieta clamancia Emme uxoris Galfridi de Ryueshale de una pecia prati q' vocatur le Cope Sudbury iij<sup>a</sup> (14th cent.)

36. Grant from Robert Schep of Melford to Richard of Clare of Sudbury and Johanna his wife, the heirs of Richard and to whomever they may grant, leave, sell or assign them, for five marks in cash (*premanibus*), of one messuage in the vill of Sudbury, lying between the tenement of Walter of Belchamp and the barn of William Tebaud, and abutting at one end on the field called *le Teynturfeld* and on the other on the king's highway going from *Sturhellestrete* towards *Croftstrete*; and of a yearly rent of 10d, namely of 8d from William Thebaud, made up of 3d William owes for a barn leased to him by William Schep and 5d for tenter-yards (*tentor(ias)*) he holds in the field of *Teynturfeld* in Sudbury, 1d from Walter of Belchamp for a tenement next to Walter's tenement mentioned above, and 1d from Gilbert de Aqua for..(ms. illegible) leading to *Teynturfeld*. Given at Sudbury, July 1294.

Data apud Subyr'.... festum Sancti Jacobi apostoli anno regis Edwardi filii regis Henrici vicesimo secundo. Hiis testibus Roberto.... Gilberto de Aqua. Waltero de Bellocampo Willelmo Thebaud Roberto de Lyketon' Willelmo le Bere Johanne... de Neuton' Rogero le Barow. Ricardo Lygon. Ricardo clerico et multis aliis.

> WAM 20811, 23.5 × 16 cm; remains of slits for seal tag; stained by damp and holed.
> Endorsed: Sudbury (14th cent.?): other endorsement damaged.

37. Grant in indenture form from Simon, prior of St Bartholomew's to Henry Schingel of Sudbury, his heirs, grantees, legatees, vendees and assigns, in return for a sum of money (*unam porcionem pecunie*) of a piece of land (*unam placiam terre*) in the hamlet of Holgate in the vill of Sudbury lying between the tenement of Amaunde between the bridges of Sudbury on one side and of Henry himself on the other, abutting at one end on the priory's meadow and on the other on the king's highway to St Edmund's; at an annual rent of 8d, 4d at Easter and 4d at Michaelmas; saving access to the priory's meadow for carrying hay. 29 June 1299.

Hiis testibus Thoma de Sturhill'. Roberto de Sancto Quintino. Hugone Gauge. Willelmo de Meudon'. Galfrido de Netlisted'. Galfrido de Mel. Alexandro Cokelin. et aliis. Data die apostolorum Petri et Pauli anno Rengni Regis Edwardi vicesimo septimo.

> Both parts of the chirograph survive:
> WAM 20812, 18.9 × 15.6 cm.
> Seal on tag: vesica, green wax, 5 × 3.2 cm; a standing figure. S' PRIORAT' S; BARTHOLOMI SVBIR
> Endorsed: Holgat' (late 13th cent.)
> WAM 20813, 18.9 × 15.2 cm.
> Seal on tag, round, green wax, 1.5 cm, impression indistinct.
> Endorsed: Holgat' (contemporary). The word cut through is CIROGRAFVM

38. Quitclaim by Alexander son of Richard (Paulyn) of Sudbury to Brother Nicholas of Ware, prior, and the convent of St Bartholomew's in pure and perpetual alms, in return for half a mark of silver in cash (*premanibus*), of a

yearly rent of 10d from two pieces of land formerly given them by the said Alexander as is contained in the charter of enfeoffment (*carta feoffamenti*) which he made for them. Late thirteenth century, before 1286.

Hiis testibus. Domino Hugone Talemache milite. Willelmo de Meleford. Ada Wyth. Alano Boydin. Roberto Yue. Galfrido Thom'. Willelmo filio Elie. Hugone Gauge. Gilberto de Aqua. Thoma de Sturhill'. Thoma filio Philippi. Gilberto Thoke. et aliis.

> WAM 20858, 17.5 × 11.4 cm.
> Seal on tag: round, green wax, 2.6 cm; a standing robed figure (female?) with hawk on left hand and hound at feet. S' ALEXANDRI FILII RICARDI
> Tag: a reused slip cut from a charter, reading as follows:
> Sciant...lm' de Subyr'...concessi et hac presenti ca...omnino quiet' clamaui... deo et (interlineation illegible) mon...Subir' et fratre Nicholao de Ware prior eiusdem...seruientibus...in puram
> Endorsed: (c.1300?) Carta Alexandri Paulyn de .x. denariis annui redditus in Suthbyr' iiijᵃ
> Date: William son of Elias was dead by 1286. Many witnesses occur in 1282 (no. 31).
> Note: the rent quitclaimed is that reserved in nos 21–2.

39. Grant from Alexander son of Richard (Paulyn) of Sudbury to William de Holgate and whomever he may give, leave, sell or assign it, in return for four marks in *gersuma*, of two acres in the field towards Holgate between the land of Stoke by Clare priory and the lane (*venella*) going from Sudbury to St Barthlomew's, one end abutting on Alexander's land, the other on the king's highway; paying 2½d at Michaelmas and 2½d at Easter; warranty against all men and women. Late thirteenth century.

His testibus. Willelmo filio Warini. Micaele filio Walteri. Gilleberto filio Audre. Willelmo de Aketon Thoma de Holgat'. Ricardo fratre eius. Roberto molendinario Thoma de Kentewell'. Ricardo filio Mathei. Waltero filio Dauid. W(illelmo) de Lausele et aliis.

> WAM 20859, 20.3 × 8.4 cm. Slits for seal tag.
> Endorsed: Carta Alexandri filii Ricardi de Sudb.. de duabus acris terre ijᵃ Holgate (14th cent.)
> Date: the donor (see no. 38).

40. Grant from Robert Pathogg, miller, to Robert de Kyrkele of Sudbury, his heirs and to whomever he may grant, leave, sell or assign it, in return for a certain sum in cash (unspecified), of 5s annual rent payable half at Michaelmas and half at Easter, from a messuage in the hamlet of Holgate in the vill of Sudbury, lying between the holdings of Richard of Polstead (*Polsted*) and Richard Corde; warranty against all people. Given at Sudbury, 21 September 1310.

Data apud Subyr' die dominica proxima post festum Sancti Matthei Apostoli. anno regni Regis Edwardi filii Regis Edwardi quarto. Hiis testibus. Willelmo de

Maldon. Jacobo de Peyton' Galfrido Denyel. Thoma de Sparham. Johanne
Clerebaud. Ada Pasce. Ricardo de Polsted' et multis aliis.

WAM 20846, 24.4 × 10.7 cm. Slits for seal tag.
Endorsed: Carta Roberti de Kyrkeleye de vs. redditu in Holgate (14th cent.)

41. Grant from Robert de Kirkele of Sudbury to Isabelle Rockelond of *Le
Westtoun* of Yarmouth (*Gernemouthe*), her heirs and to whomever she may
grant, sell or assign them, in return for a certain sum of money in cash, of a built
messuage in Sudbury between the messuage formerly of Thomas Warin and the
lane (*venella*) called *Stiuardeslane*, abutting at one end on the street leading from
the market towards the Friars Preachers, and at the other on the said lane; and
also of six pieces of arable land in Sudbury, lying as follows:
(1) at the great ditch between (land) formerly of William Turk and of Adam
Pake, abutting one end on the ditch, the other on land formerly of Robert of
Barton (*Bertone*);
(2) between land of Stephen of Chilton (*Chiltone*) and formerly of Richard de
Wilebi, abutting on the road from Sudbury to Cornard (*Cornerthe*) and on the
meadow of *dominus* Thomas le Grei;
(3) between the land of Mr Richard Cokelin and of Richard de Polstead
(*Polstede*), abutting on the land once of Ralph of Halstead and on the street
(*strata*) from Sudbury to Cornard;
(4) between the land formerly of the earl of Gloucester and that of Thomas
Michel, abutting on the land of the said earl and on the road from Sudbury to
Lavenham;
(5) between the land of Mr Robert Plomer on both sides, abutting on the land
formerly of Thomas Michel and that of the prior of St Bartholomew's;
(6) between the land of Sarah of the Water (*Sarra de aqua*) and that of Mr Robert
Plomer, abutting on the land formerly of Thomas Michel and on that of William
of Dedham;
also a piece of meadow lying in the meadow of Holgate between those of Mr
Richard Cokelin and Thomas of Parham, abutting on the other road from
Sudbury to Melford and on the meadow formerly of Henry de Dote;
all to be held with hedges and ditches and free entry and exit of the chief lords of
the fee for the service customarily due, with warranty against all people. Given
at Sudbury, 24 July 1318.

Hiis testibus Willelmo de Maldone. Willelmo Persoun. Thome de Parham
Roberto de Riweshale. Simone de Birthone. Ricardo de Polstede Rogero le Bret.
Gilberto de Clar' Willelmo de Eston et aliis. Data apud Suberiam die Jovis in
vigilia Sancti Jacobi Apostoli Anno Regni Regis Edwardi filii Regis Edwardi[1]
duodecimo.

[1] Edwardi interlined

WAM 20847, 23.2 × 24.1 cm; tag for seal.
Endorsed: Carta Roberti de Kyrkele de Suberia de quodam mesuagio cum sex peciis
terre arabilis et una pecia prati concess' Isabelle Rochelond faciend' domino feodi
servicia debita et consueta. (14th cent.)

42. Letter containing notes of exceptions and justification to be exhibited by principal or substitute proctors of St Bartholomew's priory in the tithe dispute with Mr Warin of Fulbourn, rector of St Gregory's, Sudbury: forms of words to be used by the proctor in court; notes of proctor's speech claiming that the prior was in legitimate possession of the tithes at issue as his right, and that this was known to all in the neighbourhood, and asking for Warin to be condemned to perpetual silence and to pay expenses.

Mr Richard of Gloucester's advice: the justification need not be proposed until a trial date is fixed. (The proctor) will have two delays, one for consultation and one to propose exceptions. Richard not knowing what was last done, he did not make a dilatory exception apart from those mentioned above; the justification should be proposed when a day is fixed. Written at Westminster on All Souls day, at the ninth hour. Early fourteenth century, before 1323.

> WAM 20770, 23.1 × 21.4 cm. No sealing.
> Endorsed: Gloucestr' Contestacio litis per inde iustificacio.....
> Date: this litigation leads up to the composition of 1323, nos 44–5. See above, p. 3.

43. Memoranda in the lawsuit between the rector of St Gregory's, Sudbury, and St Bartholomew's: to see if the 3½ acres held by the rector by virtue of an old agreement are measured by the perch of 8½ feet or not; to see by trustworthy men elected with the agreement of the parties how much of the prior's land the rector has dug, so that the boundaries can be established; to see if one acre of the rector's is better than one of the prior's, or equivalent, and which could make up the difference; to see secretly and cautiously which pieces of the prior's demesne land in arable and pasture should not be tithed, and to specify their names without measurements; this to be done without a final decision, and to be put in writing. Early fourteenth century, before 1323.

> WAM 20772, 19.9 × 9.3 cm. No sealing or endorsements
> Date: leads up to the agreement of 1323 (no. 45).

44. Inspeximus by (Robert de Langley) prior and the chapter of Norwich of a ratification by John (Salmon) bishop of Norwich of a composition between Mr Warin de Fulbourn, rector of St Gregory's church, Sudbury, on one side, and (William Kirtlington) abbot and the convent of Westminster and Brother Simon de Henlegh, prior or custodian (*custos*) of St Bartholomew's priory, Sudbury on the other, touching the greater and lesser tithes from lands and animals of the priory claimed by the rector to be within the bounds of the parish, and by the prior to be the ancient possession of his house. The priory is to take tithes anciently taken as follows, and from the lands they cultivate themselves or have in their own hands; extents are by common estimation, not by measurement.

Arable: from two pieces of land called *Feirelond*, 14 acres, before the west gate of the cell to left and right; from 8 acres immediately below the cell's garden from the south side to the earl of Gloucester's wood; from the whole field of *Hipemere*, 40 acres and more, both sides of *Hipemere* towards *le*

*Portewey* and towards the said cell except for 5 acres adjoining the middle ditch of the field on the west; from 3 acres 3 roods by the *Portewey*, between it and the land of Simon de Berton; from 2 acres 1 rood towards the *Portewey* between the land of the said Simon and that of Simon de Grangia; from 9 acres below *Setecopp'* from the east side of the cell's garden to *Hipemere* field, and from the north side to the road from Sudbury to *Northho*; from 6 acres on *Setecopp'*; from all of *Ridelescroft*, containing 4½ acres; from all of *Florelond*, 5 acres; from all of *Copehod*, 2½ acres; from 7½ acres in *Meleford* field towards *Barfoteswell* lying between the monks' land and that of William de Malton.

Meadows: in *le Prioresmedwe*, from all the meadow in the enclosure of the Stour nearest to Borley (*Borlegh*), 4½ acres, and from 4 acres 1 rood in the enclosure nearest the king's road.

And all the lesser tithes from their pastures and gardens within St Gregory's parish; and major and minor tithes from 2½ roods and 12 perches below the earl of Gloucester's wood to the north, at the east end of *Hipemere* field; and from 3 roods 8 perches on *Setecopp'* west of *Ridelescroft*.

In exchange the abbot and convent gave the rector the greater tithes of other pieces of their ancient non-titheable land: from 3 roods below the earl's wood to the north in a valley between the lands of Nigel Thibaud and Mariota le Dist(er); from 5 acres in *Hipemere* field by the middle ditch on the west; from 1 acre called *Prikesacre*; from a piece called *le Longacre*; from 2 acres called *Boydeneslond*; from 5 acres called *Brodedole*; from two pieces containing 1½ acres next to *Brodedole* towards Melford on either side of the land of Mariota le Dist(er); from 5 acres in Melford next to *Barfoteswell*, with the monks' land on one side and the bondage of Melford on the other; from a half-acre plot of land in the meadow close called *le Prioresmedwe* by the king's road.

Meadow: 1 acre 1 rood in *Sudburimedwe*; in *le Prioresmedwe* from 3 roods, formerly of Geoffrey de Riveshal' in the enclosure of the king's road towards the mill pond of *Holegate*, from 1 acre formerly of Pat of Holgate, and from 1 acre formerly of Took of Acton; from 1 acre below *Meleford*; and from all land and meadow in the parish that the priory may acquire in future.

Given at Westminster, 5 May 1323 by the rector, and at Norwich vii Kal. Aug. (26 July) 1323 by the bishop. The inspeximus is dated in the chapter house at Norwich, v. Id. Sept. (9 September) 1323.

WAM 20848, indenture, 50.2 × 36.9 cm; torn slit for seal tag.
Endorsed: Ratificacio Prioris et Capituli de Norwyco super ordinacionem episcopi... inter priorem de Sudbur' et rectorem Sancti Gregori ibidem... Sudbury (14th cent.)

45. Inspeximus by (Robert de Langley) prior and the chapter of Norwich of a ratification by John (Salmon) bishop of Norwich of a composition between the parties of no. 44 touching a dispute over the measurement of 3½ acres which Mr Warin de Fouldone, the rector of St Gregory's Sudbury, claimed to hold of the abbot and convent of Westminster and the prior or custodian of St Bartholomew's Sudbury; and over injuries and damages sustained by the rector in his lands below the earl's wood and in the field of *Setecopp'* from

grazing by the prior's animals, about which they had often previously gone to law. The abbot, convent, prior and their successors concede and demise to Mr Warin de Fouldone and his successors 2 roods and 10 perches of arable land towards Holgate lying between the lands of Robert le Plomer and William de Dedham; and 1½ acres of their ancient non-titheable land towards Holgate opposite the monks' cross lying between the road from Sudbury to *Northho* on one side and the land of Simon de Berton on the other, and between the said Simon's land and that of William de Dedham at either end. They receive in exchange 2 roods and 12 perches lying below the earl of Gloucester's wood to the north at the west end of *Hipemere* field, and 3 roods 8 perches on *Setecopp'* west of *Ridelescroft*. On any future attempt to call this agreement into question £10 will be payable to the other party.
Given as no. 44.

> WAM 20849, indenture, 46 × 23.9 cm.
> Seal on tag, round, 8.3 cm; Norwich cathedral priory; almost perfect impression; illustrated in VCH *Norfolk* ii, opposite p. 326.
> Endorsed: Finalis concordia.... de Sudbury et rectorem Sancti Gregorii.. decimis terrarum ibidem ad... prioratus et conventus ac etiam ratificacio prioris et capituli de Norwyco... (contemporary); Sudbury (15th cent.)

46. Lease from Thomas de Maldon of Sudbury to John de Eye of Sudbury and his assigns of a piece of land at Holgate in Sudbury next to the lands of John Knevet and abutting on the said Thomas's land, from the following Michaelmas for John's lifetime, at a yearly rent of one peppercorn at Christmas for the first 5 years and afterwards 20s annually; if John should die within five years, his heirs, executors or assigns may hold the land for the rest of that period; warranty, for the term, against all people. Given at Sudbury on Wednesday after St John Baptist's day, 10 Edward III (24 June 1336).

> WAM 20865, indenture, 24.9 × 13 cm (max.). Slits for seal tag.
> Endorsed: si carta ...tunc cartas...tenement' in Sturmer (14th cent.)

47. Quitclaim from Mr Simon son of Nigel Thebaud of Sudbury to Nigel Thebaud, Sarah his wife and Nigel's heirs of all lands and tenements which he had by gift from Nigel his father in the vills of Sudbury and Melford. Given at Sudbury, 6 December 1345.

Hiis testibus. Johanne Kneuet. Johanne de Place. Johanne Thebaud et aliis. Datum apud Sudbery die Lune ante festum Sancti Nicholai Episcopi. Anno regni Regis Edwardi tercii post conquestum decimo nono.

> WAM 20866, 28.7 × 5.4 cm.
> Seal on tag, shield, red wax, 2 × 1.5 cm; a talbot rampant. Inscription illegible. No endorsement.
> Note: this is the Simon of Sudbury who later became archbishop of Canterbury – see above, p. 3; for the Thebaud chantry, see above, pp. 3–4.

48. Copy of a grant by Simon (de Bircheston) abbot and the convent of Westminster to Elizabeth de Burgh, Lady of Clare, Nigel Teboud and Sarah his wife, Mr Simon Teboud, Robert Teboud and John Teboud, in return for their gifts and largesses bestowed on the abbey's cell at Sudbury, of participation in all the spiritual benefits to be obtained in the said abbey, its cells and the churches confederated with it, especially a daily mass celebrated for them at the cell of Sudbury by a monk of the house; on news of the death of each of the beneficiaries every priest of the house and the aforesaid churches shall celebrate special masses as for a brother of the house, and those in minor orders shall recite the usual psalms; the beneficiaries' names will be entered in the abbey's *martilogium*, and after their death their names will be circulated for absolution to all the chapters of England and Wales, with the name of the next monk to die. Given in the Chapter House at Westminster, 4 May 1349.

WAM 20867, 27.8 × 13.2 cm; no sign of sealing.
Note: on the dorse is no. 126, q.v.

49. Grant from Nigel Tebaud of Sudbury (*Sudbery*) to Henry, rector of Brundon (*Brumdon*), Thomas de Lynton, chaplain, Stephen Waryn, chaplain, John Tebaud, John Lygoun, John de Morton, John Dodecote and Richard Rook, their heirs and assigns, of 80 acres of land and meadow in the hamlet of Holgate in Sudbury; the land lies between the road which goes from the stone cross towards the wood of *Kyngeswode*, and the road called *le Melnewey* leading from the mill of Holgate towards Acton, abutting at one end on the king's highway from Melford to Sudbury, and at the other on the land of the cell of St Bartholomew's; the meadow lies in *le Northmedwe* next to the cell's meadow; to be held of the chief lord of the fee for the service due (unspecified); warranty against all people. Given at Sudbury, 19 May 1349.

Testibus. Roberto de Ryueshale. Johanne Waryn Johanne atte Berne Johanne de Eye Benedicto le Spycer et aliis. Dat' apud Sudbery predictam die dominica proxima ante festum Sancti Dunstani anno regni regis Edwardi tercii a conquestu vicesimo tercio.

WAM 20868, 29.2 × 10.3 cm.
Seal on tag, round, red wax, 2.1 cm; a geometrical design.
Endorsed: (14th cent.) De ....aria Nigelli ..... Sudbury ijᵃ

50. Grant from Mariota widow of Walter le Dextere of Sudbury to Henry, rector of Brundon (*Brumdon*), Thomas de Lynton, chaplain, Stephen Waryn, chaplain, and John de Murton, their heirs and assigns, of two pieces of land in Sudbury; warranty against all people. Given at Sudbury, 7 July 1349.

Hiis testibus Nigello Thebaud Roberto de Ryueshal Johanne Lytel de Melford' Henrico le Ne.. ...Rougheued Johanne Allone Johanne Ryueshal et aliis. Dat' apud Sudbery die dominica proxima post festum translacionis Sancti Th(ome anno regni) regis Edwardi tercii post con(questum vic)esimo tercio.

WAM 20869, damaged and stained, originally c.22 × 15.2 cm; tag for seal; endorsement illegible.

51. Quitclaim from Thomas son of Walter le Dextere of Sudbury to Henry, rector of Brundon (*Brumdon*), Thomas de Lynton, chaplain, Stephen Waryn, chaplain and John de Murton of land in Sudbury given them by Mariota, widow of the above Walter and mother of Thomas. Given at Sudbury, 7 July 1349.

Hiis testibus Nigello Thebaud Roberto.... (Johanne) Allone et aliis. Dat' apud Sudbery die dominica proxima post f(estum translacionis Sancti) Thome anno regni regis Edwardi tercii post conquestum vic(esimo tercio).

> WAM 20870, damaged and badly stained, originally 20.5 × 11.7 cm; sealing uncertain.
> Endorsed: (14th cent.) Sudbury ijᵃ

52. Quitclaim from John de Morton to Richard Rok, senior, of the vill of Westminster, of his rights in 80 acres of land and meadow in the field of Sudbury in the diocese of Norwich, formerly belonging to Nigel Tebaud of Sudbury. Given at Sudbury, 25 January 1356.

Hiis testibus Johanne de Reuishale Johanne Lygoun Johanne Waryne Stephano de Chilton' Ricardo Aboi' et aliis. Dat' apud Sudbery die veneris proxima post festum conversionis Sancti Pauli apostoli anno regni regis Edwardi tercii post conquestum tricesimo.

> WAM 20871, 26.7 × 9.1 cm; slits for seal tag.
> Endorsed: iijᵃ

53. Grant from Robert ate Place of Sudbury in free alms to Simon de Langham, abbot of Westminster, and the prior of St Bartholomew's, which priory is a cell of the said abbey, of license to acquire and possess the lands and tenements which Nigel Thebaud acquired in the hamlet of Holgate in Sudbury, and given by him to John Thebaud his son, John Lygoun, Henry de Dodelintone rector of Brundon (*Braundone*), John de Mortone and Richard Rook, senior, of Westminster, to enfeoff the said abbot and prior to found one chantry (*cantoria*) in the said priory, and to celebrate therein for the souls of the above Nigel, his parents and kindred for ever; saving to himself, Robert, the rents due from the lands. Given at Sudbury, 13 July 1357.

Hiis testibus Johanne de Reuishale Thoma de Ber Johanne Gotte, Johanne Alone Stephano de Chiltone Rogero ate Roche et aliis multis. Dat' apud Sudbery die iovis in festo Sancte Margarete virginis anno regni regis Edwardi tercii a conquestu tricesimo primo.

> WAM 20872, 28.5 × 11.8 cm; tag for seal.
> Endorsed: viijᵃ

54. Quitclaim from John Thebaud, son of Nigel Thebaud of Sudbury to Richard Rok of the vill of Westminster of 80 acres of land and meadow in the field of Sudbury in Norwich diocese formerly belonging to the above Nigel, reserving a yearly rent of 6d. Given at Sudbury, 13 July 1357.

Hiis testibus Johanne Reuishale Johanne Lygoun Johanne Warine Stephano de Chilton Ricardo Aboi et aliis. Dat' apud Sudbery die iovis in festo Sancte Margarete anno regni regis Edwardi tercii post conquestum tricesimo primo.

> WAM 20873, 28.8 × 8.5 cm.
> Seal on tag, round, red wax, 2.3 cm; a shield within a pattern with 4 small supporters; device indecipherable, inscription illegible.
> Endorsed: iiij

55. Grant from Richard Rook, senior, of the vill of Westminster to Simon, abbot of Westminster and the prior of St Bartholomew's of 80 acres of land and meadow in the field and meadow of Sudbury in the hamlet of Holgate, the bounds described as in no. 49; which lands and meadow Nigel Tebaut of Sudbury gave to the said Richard to enfeoff the above abbot and prior, for the souls of the said Nigel and all his relatives, to hold of the chief lord of the fee for the service due (unspecified); warranty against all people. Given at Sudbury, 24 July 1357.

Hiis testibus Johanne Gotte, Thoma de Bury, Johanne de Reueshal', Ricardo de Burgh', Stephano de Chilton, Johanne Prentys et aliis. Dat' apud Sudbery vicesimo quarto die mensis Iulii. anno regni regis Edwardi tercii a conquestu tricesimo primo.

> WAM 20874, 25.4 × 11.8 cm.
> Seal on tag, fragment, pink wax, 2.5 × 1.8 cm: see no. 56.
> Endorsed: (14th cent., apparently on an erasure) ..que quidam terram et ... nuper habui ex dono et feoffamento......Thebaut de Sudbury xxiv$^{to}$ (post medieval?) Sudburye

56. Grant from Richard Rook, senior, of Westminster to Abbot Simon and the convent of Westminster of 80 acres of land at Sudbury, in Holgate hamlet, described as in no. 49, which land was given to Richard by Nigel Thebaut of Sudbury; performing the service due (unspecified) to the chief lords of the fee; warranty against all people. Given at Sudbury in the county of Suffolk, 24 July 1361.

Hiis testibus Johanne Gotte Thoma de Bury Johanne (de Reues)hale Stephano (de C)hilton Johanne Prentys et aliis. Dat' apud Sudbery in comitatu Suff' vicesimo quarto die Iulii anno regni regis Edwardi tercii post conquestum tricesimo quinto.

> WAM 20876, 26.6 × 11.6 cm.
> Seal on tag, round, 2.4 cm (cracked), pink wax; heraldic, a bend with an uncertain charge in sinister chief; * IEO ...... DEV..
> Endorsed: ix$^{a}$

57. Power of attorney from Joan Lytil of Sudbury, executrix of the will of John Lytil her husband, to John Glouere her father, to receive in her name all and each of the goods and chattels of, and debts due to, her said husband within the vill or elsewhere in Suffolk.
Given 20 October 16 Richard II (1392).

> WAM 20883, 26.1 × 8.3 cm; tongue for seal. No endorsement.

58. Notification from William Merssh, *litteratus mandatarius* and deputy of William, abbot of St Albans and conservator of the rights and privileges of the abbot and convent of Westminster, to the abbot of St Albans that he has in obedience to his mandate (quoted in full, addressed to Mr Robert Moreshom, notary public, Richard Okle, William Merssh, John Mersshe and Thomas Bevereche, and dated 4 November 1418), personally cited Geoffrey, Warden of St Gregory's College, Sudbury, to appear in St Alban's abbey and answer for abducting the tithes arising from lands within the boundaries of St Gregory's parish belonging to the cell or priory of St Bartholomew's, Sudbury; but that he has failed to cite Robert Spicer, vicar of the said college, as he could nowhere be found. Sealed by the Examiner General of the court of Canterbury.
Given at London, 24 November 1418.

> WAM 20886, 36.5 × 23.7 cm; sealing probably on tongue, cut away. No endorsement.

# ACTON

59. Grant from Robert *Magister*, son of Godric, of Acton (*Aketun*), to St Bartholomew's with the assent of Richard his son of 2½ acres *En la scrib* together with his body for burial; and confirmation of his old grant of 1 acre in *Haselhangra* and of the land of Alwin Red; Richard and his heirs will acquit the service due to the king and the lord. Late twelfth century.

Notum sit omnibus tam presentibus quam futuris quod ego Robertus magister de Aketun filius Godrici consilio et assensu Ricardi heredis mei do et concedo et hac presenti carta mea confirmo deo et Sancto Bartholomeo et monachis ibidem famulantibus cum corpore meo duas acras terre et dimidiam enlascrib que iacent iuxta terram Alwini Red in oriente pro salute mea et Ricardi heredis mei et pro anima uxoris mee et omnium antecessorum meorum liberam et quietam ab omni seruicio inperpetuum. Preterea do et concedo predictis monachis antiquam donacionem meam scilicet unam acram prati in Haselhangra et terram predicti Alwini Red. Et Ricardus filius meus et heredes sui omnes consuetudines quas a predictas donationes pertinent contra regem et dominum suum et omnes alios warantizabit et defendet. His Testibus. Roberto Capellano de Aket(un). Galfrido filio eius. Willelmo Nerbod. Roberto de Witzand. Roberto de Futipo. Willelmo Ridel. Adam filio Cristine. Loqre' filio Absalonis. et multis aliis

> WAM 20760, 13.5 × 14.2 cm. Tag for seal consisting of a single strip of parchment 32.9 cm long, a reused document, on one side reading: Notum sit uniuersis matris ecclesie filiis. quod ego Johannes filius Benedicti dedi... presenti carta confirmaui
>
> Endorsed: Rob' Magr' de Aketun'. de ij acris terre en la scrib et j acra prati in haselangra jª (late 13th cent.)
>
> Date: for John son of Benedict see no. 2. Richard *filius magistri* occurs in no. 18, before 1223.

60. Promise from Gilbert son of Robert Toke of Acton (*Aketon*) for himself, his heirs and assigns, to the prior of St Bartholomew's to defend at his own expense the three acres of land with appurtenances in Acton purchased by him from Gregory, prior of St Bartholomew's, in case any heir of Walter Wrau should implead them at any time in any court; and should it happen that any heir of Walter should establish title to the land in court, the prior at the time shall return the 5s Gilbert gave for the land. Gilbert and his assigns will not sell or pawn the land to any Jew, or give it to any religious house except St Bartholomew's. Late thirteenth century.

Hiis testibus. Giliberto filio Aldre. de Suthbiri. Michaele filio Walteri. Thoma le Ruter. Rogero clerico. Adam de Withes Alano Pokestreng'. Adam le Rus. Elys filio Martin et multis aliis.

WAM 20778, 16.6×7.5 cm.
Seal on tag: vesica, green wax, 3.1×2 cm; a dragon. +SIGILL' GILEB': THOHE
Endorsed: Carta de Aketon' (late 13th cent.)
Date: Gilbert Toke and Adam With occur in the 1280s (nos 31, 96).

# BRADFIELD

61. Grant from Robert le Mul to Nicholas Ording, his heirs and assigns, in return for 16d in *gersuma*, of 2d due to Robert from Nicholas when scutage is levied at 20s, for a piece of land in Bradfield (*Brodfeld*) which Constantine le Fiket holds of Nicholas at a yearly rent of 4d; Nicholas will pay Robert one peppercorn when scutage is placed on the king's land. Warranty against all men and women. Late thirteenth century.

Hiis testibus. Roberto de Vall'. Roberto de Wafere. Simone le Bret. Willelmo filio Rogeri. Roberto filio Hugonis. Mauricio de Chelueston'. Tomas miles. Thoma Blanche. Godefrido de Chelueston' et aliis.

WAM 20832, 19 × 7.7 cm. Slit for seal tag.
Endorsed: jᵃ
Date: Nicholas Ording was dead by 1303 (see nos 87–8, and above, p. 11).
Note: it is not known which Bradfield (St Clare, St George or Combust) this refers to.

# CHEDBURGH

62. Grant from Philip of Kedington to John Hamund of Chedburgh (*Chetebere*), his heirs and assigns, for an annual rent of 4d to the chief lord payable equally at Easter and Michaelmas at the tenement called *Biggyng*, of a garden called *Valleyserd* in the vill of Chedburgh, between the common and the land of Reginald Sparwe, abutting at one end on the garden of John Alston, and at the other on the garden of the said John Hamund. Given at Chedburgh, 1 August 1400.

Hiis testibus Johanne Sparwe Roberto Webbe Johanne Alston Petro Jogyl Reginaldo Sparwe et aliis. Datum apud Chetebere predict' in Advincula sancti Petri anno regni Regis Henrici quarti post conquestu primo.

WAM 20885, indenture, 23.6 × 9.6 cm.
Seal on tag, red wax, fragment 1.6 × 1.3 cm.
Endorsement: (15th cent.) Chetber

# CLARE

63. Grant from John of Essex, *miles*, at the instance of Isabel his wife to St Bartholomew's in pure and perpetual alms of a rent of 5d, payable at Michaelmas and the Annunciation, from Richard del Perin in the vill of Clare; warranty against all men and women. Late thirteenth century.

Hiis testibus. Willelmo Rufo. Waltero fratre eius. Ricardo de Ponte. Ricardo carpentario. Roberto Huberd et multis aliis.

WAM 20793, 20 × 9.0 cm. Slits for seal tag.
Endorsed: Carta Johannis de Essexe militis de quinque denarios redditus in villa de Clare
Date: William Ruffus of Clare, *clericus*, and Walter his brother appear before 10 March 1289 (*Aug Friars*, no. 25). Sir John of Essex died in 1290 and was succeeded by his heir, another John (*Cal Inq PM* iv, no. 147).

64. Grant from Hubert de Montchensy to St Bartholomew's of one *summa* of wheat yearly at Michaelmas, to be received at Edwardstone; confirmation by Hubert of the gift by William of Goldingham of another *summa* of wheat each year at the same term. Early to mid-twelfth century.

Sciant presentes et futuri quod ego Hubertus de Munchanesi dedi et hac presenti carta mea (confirm)aui deo et Sancto Bartholomeo.... et monachis ibidem deo seruientibus unam summam frumenti in perpetuam elemosinam singulis annis ad festum Sancti Michaelis.... meum apud Adwardest' recipiendam pro salute anime mee et uxoris mee.............. Concedo et confirmo donationem quam Willelmus de Goldigham eidem... fecit scilicet aliam summam frumenti singulis annis ad....... ab ipso et suis successoribus secundum quod carta eiusdem testatur apud Goldingham percipiendam Et ne quis succedentium hered............-entium hanc elemosinam nostram retinere imminuere uel..... calumpnia predictis monachis exinde facere presumat per..........contestare prohibeo .....et ut rata sit hec mea donatio... gravaciones stabilis eam presenti scripti testimonio.......impressione corroborare curaui. Hiis testibus Rogero persona de Adwardest' Gregorio clerico. Hugone de Muncanesi et Roberto fratre eius. Simone de Burgate et multis aliis.

WAM 22836, 17.7 × 6.2 cm. Tag for seal. Faint endorsement illegible.
Date: for the Montchensys of Edwardstone, stewards of the honour of Eye, see Vivien Brown, *Eye Priory Cartulary* ii, 10, 58. One Hubert was a Domesday tenant of the fee of William Malet (DB 325a, 326b); the Hubert of this charter was active in 1136-7 (*Eye Priory Cartulary* i, no. 15), and the father of the Hugh de Montchensy who occurs in 1159-64 (John L. Fisher, *Cartularium Prioratus de Colne*, Essex Archaeological Society Occasional Papers i, 1946), no. 65, datable from Abbot Walkelin of Abingdon, which Hugh is probably the witness to this charter. For a third Hubert see below, no. 91. The script of this charter is early or mid-twelfth century.

# GOLDINGHAM (ESSEX)

65. Confirmation by John of Goldingham, *miles*, to St Bartholomew's of one measure (*summa*) of wheat which his ancestor William of Goldingham once gave them, to be paid yearly within fifteen days of Michaelmas, at his manor of Goldingham. Given at Goldingham, in Bulmer parish, 1 September 1359.

Dat' apud Goldyngham in parochia de Bulmere in die Sancti Egidii abbatis anno regni regis Edwardi tercii post Conquestu tricesimo tercio. Hiis testibus Domino Johanne....[1] Henrico atte Ven Thoma de Est(on) et Willelmo fratre eius Roberto Gerald Johanne le Smyht et multis aliis.

[1] Blank in ms

WAM 20875, 24.1 x 7.3 cm.

Seal on tag, round, brown wax, 2.2 cm; within a decorated circle a shield of arms, *a bend wavy*. * S' IOHANNIS DE GOLDINGHAM No endorsement.

Note: the Goldingham arms were *argent a bend wavy gules*.

# GREAT WRATTING

**66.** Quitclaim from Gilbert the smith (*Faber*) of Great Wratting (*Mangna Wratting*) to Nicholas Ording his brother, his heirs and assigns of his rights in the whole tenement formerly belonging to Wade Ording, for a payment of 18s, and half a *summa* of corn (*bladi*) a year during Gilbert's life, that is at Christmas 2 bushels of wheat and 2 of barley. Late thirteenth century.

Hiis testibus. Galfrido Curpayl. Symone le Bret. Roberto filio Hugonis. Radulpho filio Ade. Mauricio de Cheluestun'. Godefrido de Fonte Roberto Palmar' et multis aliis

WAM 20844, 19.6 × 7.5 cm.
Slits for seal tag.
Endorsed: Carta Gilberti fabri de tenemento quod fuit quondam Wade de Broccynge viii<sup>a</sup> (late 13th cent.)
Date: Nicholas Ording was dead by 1303 (nos 87–8).

# KEDINGTON

67. Confirmation from Algar of Langley and Matilda his wife, daughter of Hugh of Langley, to Harvey son of Richard of Pentlow of 1½ acres in the vill of Chilton which they gave to the church of Pentlow (Essex), to be held of the church of Pentlow at a yearly rent of 1d paid on St George's day for the health of the donors' souls and all the faithful departed; in return Henry gave Algar 20s and Matilda 4s. Mid- to late thirteenth century.

Sciant presentes et futuri quod ego Algar de Langelegh'. et Matilda uxor mea filia Hugonis de Langelegh' concessimus et hac presenti carta nostra confirmauimus Heruico filio Ricardi de Pentelowe unam acram terre arrabilis et dimidiam cum omnibus pertinentiis. quam dedimus ecclesie de Pentelowe. scilicet que iacet in villa de Cheluestun'. in Alfrichescroft cheu(er)ingoressune. inter terram Wade . et terram Willelmi Kelhod. et abbutat ad unum caput super terram Roberti Gundre. et ad aliud capud super cheminum de Langelegh. Habendam et tenendam predicto Heruico et heredibus suis de ecclesia de Pentelowe imperpetuum. libere. quiete. et in pace absque omni calumpnia. et impedimento nostro et heredum nostrorum. Reddendo inde annuatim eidem ecclesie unum denarium pro redempcione animarum nostrarum et omnium fidelium defunctorum. scilicet ad festum Sancti Georgii. pro omnibus seruiciis. querelis et demandis. Pro hac autem concessione et presentis carte nostre confirmacione dedit mihi predictus Heruicus viginti solidos. et Matilde uxoris mee, quatuor solidos. Hiis testibus. Waltero filio Humfridi. Roberto et Willelmo fratribus eius. Magistro Elys. Thoma Mauduith. Thoma de Bello Campo. Rogero Curpeil. Willelmo Wafre. Galfrido filio eius. Radulfo de Horkeslethe. Michaele de Wiueleshei. Roberto Merild'. Rogero Viteri et multis aliis.

WAM 20783, 15.2 × 10.4 cm.
Seal on tag, round, white wax varnished dark green, 4 cm; a striated fleur-de-lys. Inscription indecipherable. The seal appears to have been applied upside down.
Endorsed: Carte de Kedyngton' et Storemere. Kedington. j²
Date: Thomas de Belchamp occurs between 1262 and 1289 (*Aug Friars*, no. 10), and Walter son of Humphrey in 1263 and 1276 (*Aug Friars*, nos 8n, 26); Algar of Langley witnesses late thirteenth century charters (eg. below, nos 75, 77). Yet a Roger Curtpeil was dead by 1257 (*Essex Fines* i, 222), and the script of the document looks early to mid-thirteenth century.

68. Grant from Richard son of Godfrey de Fonte of Chilton (*Chelueston*) to William de la Tye of Chilton and to whomever he may give, sell, leave or otherwise assign it, in return for 11s in *gersuma*, of a piece of arable land in the field called *Chaluecroft* between Richard's land and that of Robert Palmar, abutting at one end on the land of Robert Scrippe; paying 1d annual rent at Michaelmas and Easter, and ¼d scutage. Warranty against all people. Late thirteenth century.

Hiis testibus. Galfrido Curpel. Radulpho filio suo. Roberto filio Hugonis. Radulpho filio Ade. Thoma le Knyt. Nicholao Ording. Roberto Palmar'. et aliis.

WAM 20829, 18.8 × 10.6 cm. Slits for seal tag
Endorsed: Carta Ricardi de Fonte de Chelueston' facta Willelmo de la Tye de eadem de j. pecia terre in Cheluescroft ijᵃ (14th cent.)
Date: Nicholas Ording was dead by 1303 (nos 87–8).

69. Grant from Hugh son of Arnald to Richard son of Ording and his heirs, in return for 3s in *gersuma*, of a piece of his meadow at *Trhittirode* stretching 13½ perches from the arable land towards the water next to Walter of Pentlow's meadow, and 12 perches next to Walter Curpeil's meadow; paying 4d annually at the Assumption and ½d per 1 scutage. Mid- to late thirteenth century.

His testibus. Robert de Pentelaue. Waltero presbitero. Roberto filio Merild. Godfrido Lordo. Osberto filio Randulfi Wade filio Ordingi. Rogero de Cheluestune. Thoma de Maldune. Rogero Dauid. Folco fratre suo et Willelmo fratre suo. Hugone filio Berardi. et multis aliis.

WAM 20860, 19.5 × 11.5 cm.
Seal on tag: round, 3.7 cm, white wax varnished brown; a bird. Inscription illegible. Endorsed: iᵃ
Date: Richard is probably the father of Nicholas Ording: see above, p. 11.

70. Grant from Robert son of Walter Curpeil to Richard son of Ording of Chilton (*Chelueston*), his heirs, and to whomever he may grant, leave or assign it except a religious house, in return for 10s in *gersuma*, of two acres of meadow which Robert holds of Augustine of Barnardiston (*Bernardestun'*) on either side of the meadow called *Thrittirodde*, one acre lying between the meadow of Ralph son of Alan of Chilton and of Algar of Langley (*Langelee*), one end abutting on the Stour, the other on the arable land; the other acre lying between the meadow of William Waffre and of the same Richard son of Ording, abutting on the Stour and the arable land; paying yearly 4d at Michaelmas and 4d at Easter; warranty against all men and women, except to religious houses. Mid- to late thirteenth century.

Hiis testibus. Rogero Curpeil. Willelmo Waffre. Tomas Curpeil. Nicholao de Pentelawe. Michaele de Wyueleshei. Petro de Cheluestune. Roberto de Bernardestun'. Hugue de Capeles de Bernardestun'. Willelmo de Sturemer. et multis aliis.

WAM 20854, 17.9 × 11.3 cm.
Seal on tag: vesica, green wax, 3.3 × 2.6 cm; a bird with a long beak. FRANGE..
Endorsement: C. de Kediton de ii. acris prati viz. de Ric' Ordyng ijᵃ
Date: as no. 69.

71. Grant from Robert Merild to Nicholas Ording, his heirs, and to whomever he may grant, sell or assign them except a religious house, in exchange for 12d in *gersuma* and a piece of meadow at *Merdesford* lying between Robert's own

meadow and that of Robert de Vallo, of two pieces of pasture at *Thritirodes*, one lying between the said Nicholas's pasture and that of Thomas Knight and the other between the said Nicholas's pasture and that of Ralph White (*Albi*), and another piece of pasture at *Lenches* between that of Nicholas and that of William Alan; Nicholas paying Robert 1d yearly, half each at Easter and Michaelmas; warranty against all men and women. Late thirteenth century.

Hiis testibus. Hugone Curpeil. Willelmo filio Rogeri. Roberto filio Hugonis. Adam de Sturemere. Mauricio de Cheluestun'. Willelmo Alan. Roberto Palmar'. Godefrido de Fonte. Ricardo Casse. et multis aliis.

> WAM 20841, 15.7 × 8.7 cm.
> Seal on tag, round, white wax, 2.7 cm; a plant motif.
> Endorsed: j³
> Date: Nicholas Ording was dead by 1303 (nos 87–8). For his transactions see above, p. 11.

72. Grant from William son of Ralph Alan of Chilton (*Cheluest'*) to Nicholas Ording, his heirs and assigns, in return for 5s in *gersuma*, of a piece of land in the field called *Stene* between that of the parson of Kedington and that of the said Nicholas, abutting at one end on the land of Robert Merild and at the other on the meadow of Geoffrey de Wafre, at a yearly rent of 1d payable at Michaelmas and the Annunciation; warranty against all people. Late thirteenth century.

Hiis testibus. Hugone Curpeil. Willelmo filio Rogeri. Roberto Mer(ild). Galfrido de Wafre. Symone. Willelmo de Fonte. Godefrido filio suo. Roberto Palmar' et aliis.

> WAM 20839, 15.7 × 8.4 cm.
> Seal on tag, round, white wax, 3 cm, a fleur-de-lys; +S' WILLELM...
> Endorsed: carta J...de una pecia terre pro j. den' redditu (late 13th cent.) iij³
> Date: Nicholas Ording was dead by 1303 (nos 87–8).

73. Grant from Adam son of Gerald of Sturmer (*Sturemere*) to Nicholas Ording, his heirs, grantees and assigns, in return for 12s in *gersuma* of a piece of land in the field called *Lullingele* next to *Le Weyestrete* towards the west, abutting at one end on the said Nicholas's land, for a yearly rent of 5d, half at Easter and half at Michaelmas, to St Peter's church, Kedington as his representative (*sicut aturnatus meus*); warranty aginst all people. Late thirteenth century.

Hiis testibus. Willelmo filio Rogeri. Roberto filio Hugonis. Berardo de Sturemere. Mauricio de Cheluest'. Willelmo de Fonte. Godefrido filio suo. Roberto Merild. Symone de Roinges. Roberto Palmar'. et aliis

> WAM 20840, 13.2 × 8.7 cm.
> Seal on tag, white wax, fragment 2.7 × 2.1 cm; a fleur-de-lys.
> Endorsed: Carta Ade filii Geroldi de Storemere de una pecia terre v³ (late 13th cent.)
> Date: Nicholas Ording was dead by 1303 (nos 87–8).

74. Quitclaim from Amabel widow of Gerold of Sturmer to Nicholas Ording and his heirs of a piece of land of her dower in the field called *Lullingele* next to *le Weistrete* towards the west; she has sworn to make no claim on the said land. Late thirteenth century.

Hiis testibus. Willelmo filio Rogeri. Roberto filio Hugonis. Berardo de Sturemere. Petro de Cheluestun'. Roberto Merild. Symone de Roinges. Roberto Palmer et alis.

WAM 20836, 14.3 × 5.1 cm.
Seal on tag, white wax, fragment 1.7 × 2.3 cm, device and inscription indecipherable. Endorsed: iiijᵃ
Date: Nicholas Ording was dead by 1303 (nos 87–8).

75. Grant from Godfrey le Lord to Nicholas Ording in return for 6s of land near that of Alan Spacking and *Poelweistrete* in Kedington at a yearly rent of 1d. Warranty against all people. Late thirteenth century.

Hiis testibus. Willelmo filio Rogeri. Petro de Cheluestun'....Roberto Merild. Algaro de Langeleye. Humfrido Champenais. Roberto Mulo....

WAM 20845, right half of charter torn away, c.11 (average) × 7.1 cm; tag for seal.
Endorsed: Carta de Kediton' jᵃ (late 13th cent.)
Date: Nicholas Ording was dead by 1303 (nos 87–8).

76. Grant from Peter of Chilton (*Cheluestun*) to Nicholas son of Richard Ording, his heirs and to whomsoever he should grant, sell or assign it except a religious house, in return for 4 marks in *gersuma*, of 3½ acres of land with its ditch and hedge lying between the land of Robert Merild and *Legestrete*, one end abutting on Peter's wood and the other on the croft of Robert White (*Albi*), at a yearly rent of 2d payable at Michaelmas and Easter and 1d for the king's scutage whether greater or less, and at each ward 1d; warranty against all people. Late thirteenth century.

Hiis testibus. Thoma de Valle. Michale de Wiueleshey. Humfrido filio suo. Willelmo filio Rogeri. Roberto filio Hugonis. Adam filio Geroldi de Sturemere. Mauricio de Cheluestun'. Willelmo de Fonte. Roberto filio Petri. Roberto Merild. Et multis aliis.

WAM 20834, 15 × 9.6 cm.
Seal on tag, light brown wax, fragment, 2.9 × c.1.6 cm.
Endorsed: De Petro de Cheuestun' de terra vocata le Stubinke. iiijᵃ
Date: Nicholas Ording was dead by 1303 (nos 87–8). 'Le Stubinge' is in Chilton in Kedington: see nos 80–2.

77. Grant from Geoffrey le Wafre to Nicholas Ording of Chilton (*Cheluest'*) and to whomsoever he wishes to give, sell, leave or assign it except a religious house, in return for a payment of 5s, and 2d annually at Easter and Michaelmas, of a piece of pasture between the pasture of Roger Curpeil and Nicholas's own,

abutting on Geoffrey's own pasture and that of the parson of Kedington (*Kedit'*). Warranty against all people. Late thirteenth century.

Hiis testibus. Mych(aele)...do filio suo. Thoma de Valle. Roberto de Brokhole. Petro de Cheluest'. Algaro de Langeleie. Roberto M(eril)d. Roberto de Harle. et multis aliis.

> WAM 20782, 15.4 × 8.5 cm. Slit for seal tag. Hole in witness list.
> Endorsed: vij$^a$
> Date: Nicholas Ording was dead by 1303 (nos 87–8).

78. Grant from Richard son of Thomas le Chint of Kedington to Nicholas Ording of Kedington and Matilda his wife, their heirs and to whomever they may give, sell, leave or assign it, in return for 14s in *gersuma*, of a piece of land in the field next to *Norchrofd* between the said Nicholas's land and that of Lecia Wennig, abutting at one end on the road (*strata*) called *le Weyestrete*, at a yearly rent of 1d at Easter and 1d at Michaelmas; warranty against all people. Late thirteenth century.

Hiis testibus. Domino Hugone Peche. Galfrido Curpayl. Symone le Bret. Roberto filio Hugonis. Radulfo filio Ade. Willelmo filio Willelmi de Sturemere. Roberto de Cheluestun'. Godefrido de Fonte. Roberto Palmar' et multis aliis.

> WAM 20862, 19 × 8.3 cm.
> Seal on tag, round, white wax varnished brown, 1.8 cm; a cross with dots between the arms. Inscription illegible.
> Endorsed: Kedyton ij$^a$
> Date: Nicholas Ording was dead by 1303 (nos 87–8). The witness list is similar to that of no. 66.

79. Grant from Jordan Merild to Nicholas Ording, his heirs and assigns, in return for 5s in *gersuma*, of a piece of meadow at *Thrittirodes* between the meadows of William Alan and Juliana Crok, abutting at one end on the River Stour and at the other on *Turpettes*, at a yearly rent of ½d at Easter and ½d at Michaelmas; warranty against all people. Late thirteenth century.

Hiis testibus. Hugone Curpeil. Willelmo filio Rogeri. Roberto filio Hugonis. Adam filio Geroldi. Mauricio de Cheluestun', Roberto Albo. Willelmo filio Radulfi Alan'. et aliis.

> WAM 20861, 14.2 × 8.8 cm.
> Seal on tag, round, white wax, 2.7 cm, six radiating petals. + S' IORD MERIL See no. 84, a different seal.
> Endorsed: iiij$^a$
> Date: Nicholas Ording was dead by 1303 (nos 87–8).

80. Grant from Jordan son of Robert Merild of Chilton (*Chelueston*) to Nicholas Ording of Chilton and whomsoever he should grant, sell or assign it except religious houses or Jews, in return for 16s in *gersuma*, of one acre of arable land in Chilton in the field called *Stubinge*, lying between the land of the said Jordan

and that of Nicholas Ording, one end abutting on *Leyes heg* and the other on the bank (*crusta*) of Robert of Newmarket (*de Novo Mercato*); paying annually to Jordan and his heirs 1d at Michaelmas and 1d at the Annunciation, and one farthing per £1 scutage; warranty against all men and women. Late thirteenth century.

Hiis testibus Hugone Curpeil. Willelmo filio Rogeri. Roberto le Wafre. Galfrido le Wafre. Willelmo de Bradefeld. Roberto albo. Symone lebret. Willelmo Alain. Mauricio de Chelueston'. Thoma Mil. et multis aliis.

> WAM 20852, 22 × 14 cm.
> Seal on tag: round, white wax varnished brown, 2.5 cm; six radiating petals. + S. IORDANI
> Endorsed: vᵃ
> Date: Nicholas Ording was dead by 1303 (nos 87–8).

81. Grant from Jordan Merild to Nicholas Ording, his heirs and to whomsoever he may grant, sell or assign it except religious houses or Jews, in return for 20s in *gersuma*, of one acre and two half roods of arable land in Chilton (*Chelueston*); the acre lies in the field called *Stubinge* between the land of Jordan and Nicholas, abutting at one end on *Leyesheg* and at the other on the bank (*crusta*) of Ralph White (*albi*); one half rood lies on *le stene* between the parson of Kedington's land and that of Geoffrey *Totus Mundus*, abutting at one end on the bank (*ripa*) leading to Sturmer and at the other on William Alain's meadow; the other half rood lies in the field next to *Nortcroft* between the lands of Geoffrey *Totus Mundus* and William Fike, abutting on the lands of the said Geoffrey and the parson of Kedington; paying annually 1d at Michaelmas and 1d at the Annunciation, and one farthing per £1 scutage; warranty against all men and women. Late thirteenth century.

Hiis testibus. Roberto de Valle. Roberto le Wafr'. Hugone Curpeil. Roberto albo. Willelmo Alain. Symone le Bret. Mauricio de Chelueston'. Thoma miles. et aliis.

> WAM 20853, 20.2 × 13.2 cm.
> Seal on tag, round, white wax varnished brown, damaged, c.2.8 × 2.5 cm; see no. 80.
> Endorsed: Kedynton' (14th cent.) vijᵃ
> Date: Nicholas Ording was dead by 1303 (nos 87–8).

82. Grant from Jordan son of Robert Merild to Nicholas Ording and to whomever he may grant, sell or otherwise let them, in return for 30s in *gersuma*, of one acre and two half-roods of land (*terra lucrabilis*) and a piece of meadow in Kedington (*Kediton*) parish at a yearly rent of 1d, payable at Michaelmas and the feast of the Annunciation. The acre lies on *le Stubinge* between the lands of the said Nicholas and Jordan, abutting on *Leyesheg* at one end and the bank of Ralph White (*Albi*) at the other; one half-rood lies on *le Stene* between the lands of the parson of Kedington and Geoffrey le Boc, abutting at one end on the Stine (*super Stinam*) and the other on Nicholas's meadow; the other half rood lies in

the field next to *Nortcroft* between the lands of Geoffrey le Boc and William le Fike, abutting on the lands of the said Geoffrey and Gilbert de Dodingherst; the meadow lies at *Zrittiroden* between those of William Alayn and Juliana Croc, abutting on the Stour (*Stura*) at one end and on *le Torpettes* at the other. Warranty against all men and women. Late thirteenth century.

Hiis testibus. Roberto de Valle. Roberto le Wafre. Willelmo filio Rogeri. Roberto filio Hugonis. Godefrido clerico. Roberto albo. Willelmo filio Radulfi Alain. Simone le Bret. Thoma miles. Mauricio de Chelueston'. Thoma le Blancheuil. et aliis.

> WAM 20822, 19.3 × 14.9 cm. Tag for seal.
> Endorsed: ij$^a$
> Date: Nicholas Ording was dead by 1303 (nos 87–8).

83. Grant from Jordan Merild to Nicholas Ording and to whomever he may give, sell, lease or assign it, in return for 16s in *gersuma* and an annual rent of 4d payable at Michaelmas, Christmas, St John the Baptist's day and the Annunciation, of a piece of arable land in the field next to *Norzcroftfeld* between the lands of Ralph White (*Albi*) and Thomas Chint, abutting on the land of Geoffrey Paty at one end and the tenement of Thomas Chint at the other as the bounds show. Warranty against all men and women. Late thirteenth century.

Hiis testibus. Galfrido Curpayl. Symon lebret. Thoma le Chint. Mauricio de Cheluestun'. Roberto Palmar' Godefrido de Fonte Godefrido Michil et multis aliis.

> WAM 20826, 19 × 11.9 cm.
> Seal on tag, round, white wax, 2.7 cm; see no. 79.
> Endorsed: C. Jordanis Merild de j. pecia terre in Kediton' vj$^a$ (c.1300)
> Date: Nicholas Ording was dead by 1303 (nos 87–8).

84. Grant from Jordan Merild to Nicholas Ording, and to whomever he may grant, sell, leave or assign them, in return for 20s in *gersuma* and an annual rent of 4d payable at Michaelmas, Christmas, the Annunciation and St John the Baptist's day, of one piece of arable land in the field next to *Norzcroft* between the lands of Thomas le Chint and Thomas Paty, abutting at one end on the land of Geoffrey Paty, at the other on the tenement of Thomas le Chint, as the boundaries (*bunde posite*) show; and a piece of meadow lying in *le zatt medwe* between the meadow of Ralph White (*Albi*) and William le Wyke, abutting on the water at one end and the pasture which belonged to Thomas de Hemenhal' at the other. Warranty against all men and women. Late thirteenth century.

Hiis testibus. Galfrido Curpayl. Symone le Bret. Thoma le Chint. Mauricio de Cheluestun'. Roberto Palmar'. Godefrido de Fonte et multis aliis.

> WAM 20825, 18.6 × 12.6 cm.
> Seal on tag, round, white wax, 2.7 cm; an 8-pointed star. ...RDANI ME... See no. 79, a different seal.
> The seal tag is a reused draft charter, mid-thirteenth century, which reads as follows:

Sciant presentes....ber de Stok' et Katerina uxor mea dedimus ...confirmamus deo/ et ecclesie Sancti Johannis Baptiste.....his ibidem deo seruientibus et seruituris ad ...pauperum [illegible suprascript correction] pro salute anime/ nostre et antecessorum nostrorum....dificiis et suis pertinenciis in villa de S.....men [suprascript, nktum] ex una parte et mesuag'
Endorsed: Kediton'. C. Jordani Merild de i pecia terre et una pecia prati. iijᵃ (c.1300)
Date: Nicholas Ording was dead by 1303 (nos 87–8).
Note: the seal tag is probably the draft of a charter to Stoke by Clare priory, dedicated to St John the Baptist.

85. Quitclaim from Walter son of William of Clopton (*Clohtone*) to Abbot Walter of Wenlock and the convent of Westminster and the prior of St Bartholomew's and their assigns, in return for 30s in cash (*premanibus*), of all rights and claims in the land and tenement formerly held by Nicholas Ording (*Hording*) and Richard his son of Walter's tenement in Kedington, saving to himself and his heirs 5s annual rent. 1283–1307, probably c.1303

Hiis testibus. Domino Johanne Carbunel. Domino Johanne de Hodebovile Domino Hugone Talemache. Domino Willelmo Giffard militibus. Willelmo Brian. Godefrido de Chelvestone. Willelmo de Grey Johanne de Peytone. Waltero filio Michaelis de Subyr'. Roberto de Bertone de eadem Thoma Giffard de Stokes. Galfrido filio Thome de Meleford'. Symone Thurgar. Johanne Peytevin de Meleford et multis aliis.

WAM 20817, 25.1 × 10.4 cm.
Seal on tag, round, dark red wax, 2.7 cm: see no. 86.
Endorsed: Quieta clamancia Walteri de Clopton'. viᵃ (14th cent.)
Date: Abbot Walter; Nicholas Ording's death was probably c.1303 (nos 87–8).

86. Quitclaim from Walter son of William of Clopton to Abbot Walter of Wenlock and the convent of Westminster and the prior of St Bartholomew's in return for 30s in cash (*premanibus*), of his rights in homage, reliefs and all service for the tenement and land late belonging to Nicholas Ording and Richard his son which is of Walter's fee in the vill of Kedington, saving 5s annual rent to himself and his heirs. 1283–1307, probably c.1303.

Hiis testibus. Domino J(ohanne) Carbonel Domino Johanne de Hodebovile Domino Hugone Talemache. Domino Willelmo Giffard milit(ibus). Willelmo Bryan Godefrido de Chelueston'. Willelmo de Grey. Johanne de Peyton'. Hugone Gauge de Subyr'. Roberto de Berton' de eadem Thoma Giffard de Stokes. Galfrido filio Thoma de Meleford Simone Schurgor. Johanne Peyteuyn de Meleford et multis aliis.

WAM 20823, 23 × 12.9 cm.
Seal on tag, round, black wax, 2.7 cm, a snowflake device. *S' WALTERI DE CLOPTON
Endorsed: Quieta clamancia Walteri de Clopton'. vᵃ (14th cent.)
Date: as no. 85.
Note: very similar to 85, but describing Walter's land as his 'fee' instead of his 'tenement'.

87. Quitclaim from Simon called le Mayster of Kedington and Emma his wife, daughter of Nicholas Ording, to the abbot and convent of Westminster and the prior and convent of St Bartholomew's and their assigns, in return for £4 in cash (*premanibus*), of all hereditary rights in the tenement which Nicholas Ording formerly had in Kedington, and which Richard son of the said Nicholas recently granted to the above abbey and priory; warranty against all people. Given at St Bartholomew's priory, 25 July 1303.

Hiis testibus domino Hugone Pecche. domino Roberto de Wyleby milit'. Jacobo de Peyton'. Hugone Gauge de Subyr'. Willelmo Duddingherst. Radulpho Curpayl. Rogero Yde. Willelmo de Goldington'. Alano Galant clerico et aliis. Dat' apud Prioratum Sancti Batholomei iuxta Subir'. die Iouis in festo Sancti Jacobi apostoli anno regni regis Edwardi filii regis Henrici tricesimo primo.

WAM 20814, 23.8 × 13.4 cm.
Two seals on tags: left, round, red wax, 2.1 cm, a fleur-de-lys; S' SIMONIS FIL' THOME
right, vesica, red wax, 3.1 × 1.6 cm, an elongated cross; S' EME FIL' N ORCIING*
Endorsed: viij[a]

88. Quitclaim from Robert Yde of Kedington and Alice his wife, daughter of Nicholas Ording, to the abbot and convent of Westminster and the prior and convent of St Bartholomew's and their assigns, in return for £4 in cash (*premanibus*), of all hereditary rights and claims pertaining to the tenement late of Nicholas Ording in the vill of Kedington, as Richard son of the above Nicholas recently gave it to the abbey and priory; warranty against all people. Given at St Bartholomew's priory, 25 July 1303.

Hiis testibus. domino Hugone Peche. domino Roberto de Wyleby. milit'. Jacobo de Peyton Hugone Gauge de Subyr'. Willelmo de Duddingherst. Radulpho Curpayl. Rogero Yde. Willelmo de Goldington. Alano Galant clerico et aliis. Dat' apud Prioratum Sancti Bartholomei iuxta Subyr' die Iovis in festo Sancti Jacobi apostoli. anno Rengni Regis Edwardi filii Regis Henrici tricesimo primo.

WAM 20815, 24.6 × 14.3 cm.
Two seals on tags: left, round, red wax, 2.8 cm, an inverted trident-shape; inscription indecipherable, many letters backwards and upside-down.
Right, vesica, red wax, 3 × 1.8 cm, a cross motif; :S' ALICIE FIL' N.. ORING
Right tag a reused piece of parchment, on inside: Noverit' me fecisse
Endorsed: C de Kedit' vij[a] (14th cent.)

89. Grant from Richard son of Nicholas Ording of Kedington (*Keditone*) to the abbot and convent of Westminster and the prior and monks of St Bartholomew's in pure and perpetual alms of a messuage in Kedington, performing the customary service due to the chief lords of the fee; warranty against all people, Jews as well as Christians. Probably 1303.

Hiis testibus. Dominis Simone filio Ricardi. Hugone Peche. Willelmo Giffard militibus. Willelmo de Hulmo. Willelmo Brian. Simone le bret. Willelmo filio

Rogeri. Roberto filio Hugonis. Willelmo filio Roberti filii Hugonis. Godefrido de Cheluestone. Roberto Morice et multis aliis.

> WAM 20857, 24.3 × 13 cm.
> Seal on tag: round, dark green wax, 2.7 cm; a bird. *S' RICAR . FIL . NICH'I
> Endorsement: Kedyngton iij$^a$ Carta de Kedintone de perquisicione fratris Nicholai de Ware (14th cent., over an erasure)
> Date: referred to in nos 87–8.

90. Grant from Walter son of William of Clopton to the prior and convent of St Bartholomew's, in return for 20s, of free access to the lands and tenements of his fee in Kedington formerly held of him by Nicholas Ording, reserving a yearly rent of 5s. Probably 1303.

Hiis testibus. Godefrido de Chelueston'. Willelmo filio Rogeri. Ricardo Casse. et aliis.

> WAM 20863, 15.2 × 6.2 cm.
> Seal on tag, fragment, 2.2 × 2.0 cm, a shield of arms, a fess.
> Endorsed: Carta fratris Nicholai de War' iiij$^a$ (14th cent.)
> Date: asociated with nos 87–9.

# MANTON

91. Grant from Bartholomew son of Arnold of Baylham with the consent of Margaret his wife, to St Bartholomew's of half a measure (*summa*) of wheat payable at Michaelmas yearly, at Manton (*Mannetun*). Late twelfth or early thirteenth century.

Sciant presentes et futuri quod ego Bartholomeus filius Arnaldi de Beylam consensu Margar(ete) uxoris mee dedi et concessi et hac presenti carta mea confirmaui deo et ecclesie Sancti Bartholomei de Suthbyr' et monachis in ibi deo seruientibus dimidiam summam frumenti. in puram et perpetuam elemosinam pro salute anime mee et uxoris mee. omniumque antecessorum successorumque nostrorum. singulis annis ad festum Sancti Michaelis de me et meis heredibus apud Mannetune sine contradictione et calumpnia recipiendam. His testibus Huberto de Munchanesi. Nicholao Pecche. Ricardo fratre eius. Galfrido de Wolweth'. Roberto filio eius. Thoma de Geddig'. Ricardo et Stephano fratribus eius. Hamone Pecche. et Radulfo fratre eius. Willelmo de Mannet'. Swift de Prest(ona) et Nicholao filio eius et multis aliis.

WAM 20762, 16.7 × 8.9 cm. Slits for seal tag.
Endorsed: Bartholomeus Grutun (early 13th cent.); unam dimidiam summam de frumento; Traudone (?) (early 13th cent.)
Date: Bartholomew of Baylham occurs in 1204–5 (*Norwich Acta* no. 352); a Hubert de Montchensy occurs from 1199 (Dodwell, *Fines* nos 281, 286) to 1230 and later (Rye, *Fines*, 31).

92. Grant from Alan Boydin of Long Melford (*Meleford*) to St Bartholomew's of a piece of land in Long Melford, at a yearly rent of 5d, half at Easter and half at Michaelmas. Early thirteenth century, before 1238.

Sciant presentes et futuri quod ego Alanus Boydin de Meleford dedi et concessi et hac presenti carta mea confirmaui deo et ecclesie Sancti Bartholomei extra Sutbir' et monachis ibidem deo seruientibus in puram et perpetuam elemosinam unam peciam terre cum pertinenciis suis in villa de Meleford, que scilicet pecia terre iacet iuxta terram dicte ecclesie Sancti Bartholomei et extendit se in longitudinem uersus orientem super terram Radulfi Le Arsoner de Sutbir' et uersus occidentem super terram Rogerii le tannur de Sutbir' et in latitudinem uersus partem borealem super terram Arnoldi le Paumer de Sutbir' et uersus partem australem super terram dicte ecclesie Sancti Bartholomei habendam et tenendam dictam peciam terre cum omnibus pertinenciis suis de me et heredibus meis in perpetuum reddendo inde annuatim mihi et heredibus meis quinque denarios ad duos anni terminos, videlicet ad Pascha duos denarios et obolum et ad festum Sancti Michaelis duos denarios et obolum pro omni seruicio, consuetudine, seculari seruicio et demanda. Et ego predictus Alanus et heredes mei warantizabimus, aquietabimus, et defendemus predictam peciam terre cum omnibus pertinenciis suis contra omnes homines et feminas dicte ecclesie Sancti Bartholomei inperpetuum. Hiis testibus domino Willelmo filio Warini tunc maiore de Sutbir' Domino Gileberto filio Adelredi Domino Willelmo Wisdelu Domino Waltero de Clopton' Roberto Wrau Helya filio Martini, Willelmo Snau Ada Winth de Meleford Thoma de Lauenham et multis aliis.

> WAM 20781, 18.2 × 14.4 cm. Seal tag.
> Endorsed: Meleford Carta Alani Boydin de Meleford (late 13th cent.) xj[a]
> Date: see no. 21 for many of the witnesses; for William Visdelu, who was dead by 1238, see no. 7.

93. Grant from Thomas son of Robert of Melford to William of Barton (*Berton'*) and to whomever he may grant, leave, sell or assign it, in return for 60s in *gersuma*, of 5 acres of arable land called *Brodedole* in Long Melford lying between the lands of Adam le Rus and William del Hel, at a yearly rent of 10d payable quarterly at St Andrew's day, Easter, the Nativity of St John the Baptist and Michaelmas, reserving the general aid of the abbot of Bury St Edmunds when it runs generally through the whole abbey (*per totam abbaciam*), as much as pertains to such a tenement of that fee in that vill; warranty against all men and women. Late thirteenth century.

Hiis testibus. Thoma Galent. Roberto Wyth. Radulpho filio Ivonis. Ada Rubeo. Rogero Dune. Michaele filio Walteri. Waltero filio David. Ricardo filio Mathei

Johanne Willeful. Roberto Wrau. Radulpho de Cavenedis. Alano Boydin et aliis.

> WAM 20820, 20.1 × 12.9 cm; tag for seal.
> Endorsed: Meleford' Carta Thome filii Roberti de Meleford' de quinque acris terre (14th cent.) $v^a$
> Date: Alan Boydin occurs in 1286 (no. 96), Thomas Galent (Galaund) in 1257–8 (Rye, *Fines*, 58).

94. Grant from Richard son of William de Theydene and Alice his wife to the prior and convent of St Bartholomew's in pure and perpetual alms of a yearly rent of 2d, payable at Michaelmas and Easter, from Alan Boydin of Melford for a piece of land in the vill of Melford, lying between the land of Geoffrey Denyel and the road to Sudbury, one end abutting on land of the said Geoffrey, the other on the king's road which goes to Ipswich. Warranty against all people. Late thirteenth century.

Hiis testibus. Galfrido filio Thome. Adam de Wythes. Roberto Yve. Alexandro pictore. Henrico Thurgor. Gilberto de Grangia. Philippo de Naptone. Alexandro Thurgor. Simone clerico et aliis.

> WAM 20828, 20.3 × 11.8 cm.
> Two seals on tags, dark reddish wax. Left: round, 2.9 cm; a six-pointed star; + S/ RICARDI: W....MEL'
> Right: vesica, fragment, 3.5 × 2.4 cm max.; a fleur-de-lys with excrescences on the stem. ...E FIL'...TE...
> Endorsed: Carta Galfridi Daniel de duobus denariis' annui redditus in Meleford' $x^a$ (14th cent.)
> Date: Alan Boydin, Robert Ive and Adam Wyth occur in the 1280s (nos 31, 96).

95. Grant from Adam de Grangia of Great Waldingfield (*Waldingfeld Mangna*) to St Bartholomew's, in return for one mark in *gersuma*, of half a piece of land in the vill of Melford between the land formerly of Gilbert Audr' on one side and that of Richard Chesters on the other, abutting at one end on the said prior's land and at the other on that of Robert Eadmund of Melford; paying yearly 1d and a clove (*clavum gariophili*) at Michaelmas; warranty against all people. Late thirteenth century.

Hiis testibus. Galfrido messor Roberto Wyne Alano Bodyn Ada Thurgor Simone Thurgor. Hugone de Grangia et aliis.

> WAM 20835, 20.5 × 10.4 cm.
> Seal on tag, round, green wax, 2.7 cm, part missing; a fleur-de-lys. *S' ADE:FIL':hVG...
> Endorsed: Meleford xiij$^a$
> Date: Adam, his father, and some of the witnesses occur in 1282 (no. 31).

96. Quitclaim from John son of Robert Wrau of Sudbury to the prior and convent of St Bartholomew's, in return for 6d in cash (*premanibus*), of one rood and a half of land in Long Melford (*Meleford*), between the land of Adam Withes

and that of the monks, abutting at one end on the land formerly of William son of Elys and at the other on the monks' land. 28 October 1286.

Hiis testibus. Hugone Gauge tunc preposito Subir'. Roberto de Berton' Thoma de Sturhelle. Johanne de Stonhus. Galfrido Heyward'. Alano Boydin. Ada Withes. Roberto Yue. Gilberto Wilek clerico et multis aliis. Carta ista erat composita die sabati proxima ante festum apostolorum Simonis et Iude anno rengni regis Edwardi quartodecimo

WAM 20810, 23 × 9.9 cm.
Seal on tag: circular, brown wax, 3 cm; an eight-pointed star. * S' I...HIS WRAV :
Endorsed: Quieta clamancia Johannis filii Roberti Wrau de Sutbyr' Meleford xiii[a]
(late 13th cent.)

97. Grant from Nicholas de Estrete of Colchester at the instance of Petronilla his wife, heiress of William de Venella, in return for 4½ marks sterling, to John, prior, and the convent of St Bartholomew's of 2½ acres in Melford called Longland, paying 4d yearly to the lords of the fee, and to him and his heirs one clove at Easter. Mid-thirteenth century.

Sciant presentes et futuri quod ego Nicholaus de Estrete de Colecestr' ad instanciam et peticionem Petronille uxoris mee et heredis Willelmi de Venella dedi concessi et hac presenti carta mea confirmavi Johanni priori ecclesie Sancti Bartholomei extra Subir' et monachis ibidem deo servientibus duas acras terre et dimidiam in villa de Meleford que vocantur Longa terra et iacent inter terram predictorum monachorum et terram Eadmundi de Meleford et abuttat in una parte super terram Jordani filii Senar' et in alia parte super viridam viam que extendit de Aketon' versus molendinum Radulphi. Habendas et tenendas de nobis et de heredibus nostris inperpetuum ipsis et successoribus eorum reddendo inde singulis annis dominis feodi qui pro tempore fuerint quatuor denarios ad duos terminos anni scilicet ad Pascha duos denarios et ad festum Sancti Michaelis. duos denarios. et mihi et heredibus meis unum clavum giloforatum ad Pascha. pro omnibus serviciis exactionibus. et demandis et cuiuscumque curie sequelis. Pro hac autem concessione donacione et huius carte mee confirmacione dederunt predicti prior et monachi quatuor marcas et dimidiam sterlingorum in gersumam. Quare ego predictus Nicholaus et heredes mei warentizabimus predictam terram cum omnibus pertinentiis suis predictis priori et monachis et eorum successoribus per predictum servicium contra omnes gentes inperpetuum. Ut autem hec mea concessio donacio et presentis carte mee confirmacio futuris temporibus robur firmitatis optineat presenti scripto sigillum meum apposui. Hiis testibus. Willelmo filio Warini. Gileberto filio Aldredi. Willelmo de Berton' Waltero filio David Ricardo Russel Ricardo filio Mathei Roberto Wrau Radulfo filio Yvonis at aliis.

WAM 20850, 21 × 15.5 cm.
Seal on tag, white wax, fragment 4 × 2.5 cm: see no. 6.
Endorsed, Carta Johannis de Rikemeresworth' monachi. Muleford. ix[a]
(contemporary).
Date: see nos 6–8.

98. Grant from Alan Boydin of Long Melford (*Meleford*) to Adam son of Hugh de Grang(ia), his heirs and to whomever he may give, sell, leave or assign it, in return for 10s in *gersuma*, of half a rood of land in the town (*villa*) of Melford, lying between his own land and the messuage of Walter Ruge, abutting at one end on his own land, and the other on the king's road leading to Rodbridge (*Radebreg'*); and grant to the same Adam of a yearly rent of 5d payable by the prior of St Bartholomew's for a tenement held of Alan in Melford, namely two acres and an annual rent of 5d from Hugh son of Arnold Palmar of Sudbury for three acres, paying yearly one halfpenny at Easter; warranty against all people. Late thirteenth century.

Hiis testibus. Ada Wyth'. Roberto Iue. Galfrido filio Thome. Willelmo Thurgor. Ricardo filio suo. Simone Thurgor. Gilberto Thoke. Ada Thurgor. Hugone de Grangia. Gilberto filio suo et aliis.

WAM 20856, 21.9 × 15.9 cm.
Seal on tag: round, white wax varnished brown, 2.3 cm, lower third missing; a fleur de lys.
Endorsed: Meleford xij[a] (14th cent.) Carta Ade de Grang. (15th cent.)
Date: Alan Boydin and many witnesses occur in 1286 (no. 96; compare no. 31).

## MIDDLETON (ESSEX)

99. Confirmation from Ralph the chaplain, son of William of Middleton, to St Bartholomew's in pure and perpetual alms of a rent of 8d in Middleton granted by his ancestors; the bearer therof shall be admitted to dine for charity's sake, lest having left the priory fasting he shall fail by the way; in case of failure to pay the monks may distrain land in the field called *Sturfeld*. Early to mid-thirteenth century.

Notum sit omnibus hoc scriptum visuris uel audituris quod ego Radulphus capellanus filius Willelmi de Middeltun' concessi et hoc presenti scripto confirmaui deo et ecclesie Sancti Bartholomei extra Suberi' et monachis ibidem deo famulantibus in puram et perpetuam elemosinam. octo denarios redditus quos antecessores mei eidem ecclesie instinctu pietatis et caritatis intuitu contulerunt. annuatim ad duos terminos solvendos. scilicet infra octavam diem festivitatis Sancti Bartholomei, quatuor denarios. et ad nativitatem domini, quatuor denarios. quos qui nomine meo uel heredum meorum terminis statutis attulerit, ad prandium caritative et benigne admittatur. ne relictus ieiunus, deficiat in uia. Si autem ego Radulphus uel heredes mei in predictorum denariorum solucione terminis predictis defecerimus licebit priori predicte domus et predictis monachis compellere nos super quandam terram iacentem in campo qui vocatur Sturfeld. inter terram que fuit Walteri de Middeltun' et terram Johannis filii Gilberti persone quondam de Middeltun'. In huius rei testimonium huic scripto sigillum meum apposui. Hiis testibus. Johanne filio Ricardi de Suber'. Giliberto filio Ricardi. Willelmo filio Ricardi. Giliberto filio Walteri. Petro filio Mathei. Johanne et Ricardo filiis Hu(m)fridi. Adam filio Stephani et aliis.

WAM 20864, 16.5 × 7.1 cm.
Seal on tag, round, greenish wax, originally 3.0 cm (part missing); a bird. S RA...LI COKELIN
Endorsed: (c.1300?) Carta de redditu viij. d. in villa de Middeltone a' G. Cokelino
Date: the first witness occurs in 1247–8 (*Essex Fines* i, 180), Gilbert of Middleton and Walter his son in 1206 (*CRR* iv, 290) and 1207 (*PR 9 John*, 177).

# STURMER (ESSEX)

100. Grant from Algar of Langley (*Langeleye*) and Matilda his wife to Nicholas Ording, his heirs and assigns of a piece of pasture at Sturmer (*Sturemere*) lying between that of Robert le Wafre and Nicholas's own, with the pasture Michael son of Alan held at its head; for a payment of 2s in *gersuma*, and a yearly rent of one halfpenny at Michaelmas; with warranty against all people. Late thirteenth century.

Hiis testibus. Willelmo filio Rogeri. Galfrido le Wafre. Roberto Merild. Adam filio Geroldi. Mauricio filio Radulfi. et aliis.

> WAM 20774, 12 × 7.2 cm.
> Seal on tag: round, white wax, damaged, 3.0 cm across; a fleur-de-lys. See no. 67.
> Endorsed: C. Algari de Langeleye de j. pecia pasture in Stormere (late 13th cent.) ij[a]
> Date: Nicholas Ording was dead by 1303 (nos 87–8). See above, p. 11.

101. Grant from Thomas son of Richard Knight (*miles*) of Chilton to Nicholas Ording, his heirs and assigns, in return for 24s in *gersuma*, of one piece of land *bondata foris* between *Aldeweystrete* and the messuage of the said Nicholas in Sturmer, at a yearly rent of 2d payable at Michaelmas and the Annunciation and one farthing per £1 scutage; warranty against all people. Late thirteenth century.

Hiis testibus. Willelmo filio Rogeri. Roberto filio Hugonis. Berardo de Sturemere. Adam de Sturemere. Roberto Merild. et aliis.

> WAM 20787, 18.1 × 4.7 cm; slits for seal tag.
> Endorsed: (late 13th cent.?) C. Thome filii Ricardi militis de Chelveston' de i pecia terre in Sturmer' iii[a]
> Date: Nicholas Ording was dead by 1303 (nos 87–8).

102. Quitclaim from Gerald son of Simon Adgar to Nicholas Ording, his heirs and assigns, in return for 6s, of a piece of meadow towards *Sturemere* which he held of Nicholas, lying between Nicholas's own meadow and that of Geoffrey de Wafre, abutting on the bank at one end and on the arable land at the other. Late thirteenth century.

Hiis testibus. Willelmo filio Rogeri de Sturemere. Adam de Stl' Geroldo de Sturemere. Roberto filio Hugonis. Berardo de Sturemere. Roberto Merild. Willelmo de Fonte. Mauricio de Cheluestun'. Roberto Palmar'. Willelmo filio Radulphi Alan'. et aliis.

> WAM 20830, 14 × 7.4 cm.
> Seal on tag, white wax, fragmentary and indistinct, 2 × 2.1 cm; a fleur-de-lys
> Endorsed: iij[a]
> Date: Nicholas Ording was dead by 1303 (nos 87–8).

# THORPE MORIEUX

103. Confirmation by Henry II to St Bartholomew's of two parts of the tithes of Ivo's demesne at Thorpe, which Ivo gave along with his body for burial, and which were confirmed by charter of Henry I. 1155–62.

Henricus rex Anglie et dux Normannie et Aquitanie et comes Andegavie Willelmo episcopo Norwicen' et omnibus baronibus suis de Suthfolk' salutem. Sciatis quod concedo et confirmo deo et Sancto Bartholomeo et monachis de Suthberia duas partes decim(arum) de Torp quam Iuo de suo dominio illic cum corpore suo libere dedit. Et precipio quod eam libere et iuste et quiete teneant sicut rex Henricus auus meus eis per cartam suam confirmavit ne inde aliquis eis iniuriam uel torturam faciat. T cancellario et comite Reginaldo apud Winton.

> BL Cotton Faustina A iii, fo 79v.
> *Mon Ang* iii, 459 no. 2.
> Date: the first witness is almost certainly Thomas Becket, chancellor from 1155 until his election as archbishop. The second witness is Reginald, earl of Cornwall.
> Note: for this gift see above, pp. 2–3.

104. Lease from Prior Gregory and the convent of St Bartholomew's to Nicholas Boydin of Thorpe (*Thorp*) of all their land in Thorpe with its appurtenances, except the tithe, for his life at a yearly rent of 5s, payable within the octave of Michaelmas; warranty against all people. Mid- to late thirteenth century.

His testibus. Johanne de Moriels. Willelmo de Hasting'. Herueo Gorge. Roberto Leffled. Osberto de Childestone. Willelmo Houel. Odone Sparhauek. Willelmo Salomon. Nicholao Nel. Herueo Beneyt. Galfrido de la Tye. Willelmo fratre suo. et aliis.

> WAM 20775, indenture, 16.5 × 7.5 cm. Tag for seal, a few tiny fragments still adhering.
> Endorsed: Cyrographum Nicholai Boidin de Thorp (late 13th cent.) ij^a
> Date: John de Morieux occurs in 1250–1 (Rye, *Fines*, 52), William of Hastings in 1272 (ibid., 127). Prior Gregory occurs in no. 60 above.

105. Certificate from the dean of Sudbury (unnamed) to N(icholas de Spina) abbot of St Augustine's, Canterbury, papal judge delegate, that he has fully executed his mandate, which is recited in full, to warn Nicholas, rector of Thorpe, Philip his chaplain, Hugh de Muriell, Hugh de Battesford, Odo Keterel, Robert Bendel, William de la Tye, William Boydin, Matilda his mother, and W. her husband of Thorpe parish, John Thurston, John de la Claye and Walter called Prik of Acton parish, to restore to the abbot and convent of Westminster the tithes, lands, rents and possessions allegedly unjustly detained by them,

failing which to cite them peremptorily to appear before the above abbot or his commissary in the conventual church of Bermondsey (*Bermundisheye*) on Friday after St Luke's day (18 October). The abbot's mandate is dated at Abingdon on St Matthew's eve (20 September) 1279. The dean's certificate is dated at Sudbury on Sunday before St Luke's day (15 October) 1279.

> WAM 20795, 21.1 × 10 cm, tongue for seal and tie.
> Endorsed: Certificacio prima (late 13th cent.)
> Note: for this and the following documents see above, pp. 2–3, 7.

106. Announcement by the precentor of Bermondsey abbey, as commissary of the abbot of St Augustine's, Canterbury, that he has appointed Monday next after the feast of........ to hear the cause between the abbot and convent of Westminster represented by Brother Richard de Dol, their proctor, and Nicholas de Wiham, rector of Thorpe, Hugh de Muriell, Hugh de Batesford, Philip the chaplain of Thorp, Robert Bendel, William de la Tye of Thorpe and others represented by their proctor, Mr Robert de Gillham, clerk. Given in the conventual church of Bermondsey on Saturday after St Luke's day (21 October) 1279.

> WAM 20796, 20.2 × 8 (max.) cm; tongue for seal, tiny wax fragment. Partly illegible through water or mould.
> Endorsed: (contemporary?) Acta Anno domini m.cc.lxx nono

107. Statement of the abbot and convent of Westminster to the judge in the case against Philip rector of Thorpe and Nicholas his predecessor for unlawfully receiving and extorting from the church and monks of St Bartholomew's two parts of the greater and lesser tithes from the lordship of the late Ivo of Thorpe, bestowed on the said church at its foundation and confirmed by kings of England, diocesan bishops and the church of Rome. Probably 1283.

> WAM 20797, 20.5 × 8 cm. Tongue with tiny fragment of seal, dark wax; tie.
> Endorsed: Libellus (late 13th cent.)
> Date: associated with nos 108 etc.

108. Certificate from the dean of Sudbury to the precentor of Bermondsey that he has fully executed his mandate, quoted in full, diligently to warn *Dominus* Philip, rector of Thorpe, to restore to the abbot and convent of Westminster before St Martin's day (11 November) their tithes in Thorpe, otherwise to cite him peremptorily to appear before the said precentor in the conventual church at Bermondsey on the next law day after St Clement's day (23 November) to answer the said abbot and convent. The mandate is dated at Bermondsey on the vigil of Sts Simon and Jude (27 October) 1283. The certificate is dated at Sudbury, on Saturday after St Martin's day (13 November) 1283.

> WAM 20798, 20.5 × 8 cm. Tongue for seal.
> Endorsed: Prima certificio de Thorp. anno domini Mo. cc. octogesimo quarto. (late 13th cent.)

109. Sentence of the precentor of Bermondsey relating to the non-appearance of Philip, rector of Thorpe Morieux and his accomplices in the suit with the Abbot and convent of Westminster concerning tithes in Thorpe. Given in the conventual church of Bermondsey on Monday after St Martin's day... Probably 1283–4.

> WAM 20799, 22.9 × 9 cm. Sealing cut away. Right half illegible through damp.
> Date: associated with nos 108 and 110.

110. Memorandum of letters sent by the precentor of Bermondsey as commissary of the abbot of St Augustine's, Canterbury, to the dean of Sudbury to publish in the churches of Thorpe (Morieux), Lavenham (*Laueham*), Brettenham (*Brethenham*) and Cockfield (*Cokefeld*) the excommunication of Philip, rector of Thorpe, and to cite him to appear in Bermondsey priory church on the next law day after the feast of Sts Philip and James (1 May) to answer in the cause between him and the abbot and convent of Westminster. Given at Bermondsey, Ides of November (13 November) 1284.

> WAM 20800, 24.1 × 7 cm; tongue for seal. Partly illegible through damp.

111. Appointment by Philip, rector of Thorpe, of John Houel and William of Thorpe to be his proctors in any lawsuits.
Sealed with the seal of the deanery of Sudbury, as his own seal is known to few. Given at Groton on St Edmund the Archbishop's day (16 November) 1283.

> WAM 20801, 18.5 × 6.8 cm; tag for seal.
> Endorsement: Procuracio (late 13th cent.)

112. Announcement of the precentor of Bermondsey, commissary of the abbot of St Augustine's, Canterbury, papal delegate in the case between the abbot and convent of Westminster, represented by their monk Richard de Dol (*Dole*), and Philip, rector of Thorpe, represented by William of Thorpe and Philip Houel, that at the request of the dean of Sudbury he has fixed the morrow of the Conversion of St Paul (26 January) for hearing and deciding the case. Given in St Saviour's church, Bermondsey on the morrow of St Clement (24 November) 1283.

> WAM 20802, 19.1 × 5.8 cm; tongue for seal.
> Endorsed: Acta secunda (late 13th cent.)

113. Certificate from the dean of Sudbury to the precentor of Bermondsey that he has fully executed his mandate (quoted) to cite peremptorily on pain of excommunication, Philip, rector of Thorpe, to appear before the said precentor in the conventual church of Bermondsey on the morrow of St James's day to answer the abbot and convent of Westminster concerning possession of the tithes in Thorpe parish. The mandate is dated at Bermondsey, on the eve of the feast of

Sts Peter and Paul (28 June) 1284, the certificate at Sudbury on Saturday after the Translation of St Benedict (15 July) in the same year.

WAM 20803, 19.7 × 10.8 cm; sealing cut away.
Endorsed: certificatio secunda (late 13th cent.)

114. Mandate from the precentor of Bermondsey, commissary of the abbot of St Augustine's, Canterbury, as papal delegate, to the dean of Sudbury to cite peremptorily Philip, rector of Thorpe, to appear before him in the conventual church of Bermondsey on the morrow of St James's day (26 July) to answer the abbot and convent of Westminster touching possession of their tithes of Thorpe parish.
Given at Bermondsey on the eve of Sts Peter and Paul (28 June) 1284.

WAM 20804, 17 × 8.2 cm; tongue for seal.
Endorsed: Secunda citacio (late 13th cent.)

115. Notice by the precentor of Bermondsey, commissary of the abbot of St Augustine's, Canterbury, that he has fined 20s, for contumacy, William of Thorpe, clerk, the proctor of Philip, rector of Thorpe, in the suit between him and the abbot and convent of Westminster, represented by Brother Richard de Dol, their fellow monk and proctor.
Given in Bermondsey abbey church on the morrow of St James's day (26 July) 1284.

WAM 20805, 17.1 × 7.5 cm; tongue for seal cut away. Unendorsed.

116. Decree of the precentor of Bermondsey, as principal commissary of the abbot of St Augustine's, Canterbury, in the suit between the abbot and convent of Westminster, represented by Brother Richard de Dol their fellow monk and proctor, and Philip, rector of Thorpe, who did not appear: the said Philip, in view of his multiple contumacy and frivolous appeals to the tuition of the archbishop of Canterbury, shall be publicly excommunicated by the dean of Sudbury and cited to appear before the said precentor on the next law day after the Nativity of St John the Baptist (24 June).
Given in Bermondsey abbey church on the Saturday after the feast of Sts Philip and James (5 May) 1285.

WAM 20806, 18.5 × 7.2 cm; tongue for seal, and tie.
Endorsed: Acta die sabbati post festum apostolorum Philippi et Jacobi Anno m.cc.lxxx. quinto. (late 13th cent.)

117. Letter from the dean of Sudbury to the precentor of Bermondsey informing him that he has diligently executed his mandate (quoted), given at Bermondsey, Ides of November (13 November) 1284, to excommunicate in the churches of Thorpe, Lavenham, Brettenham and Cockfield Philip, rector of Thorpe, and to

cite him to appear in Bermondsey priory church to answer in the cause between him and the abbot and convent of Westminster.
The date of the letter is not filled in.

WAM 20807, 18.7 × 18.6 cm; tongue for seal, and tie. Unendorsed.

118. Letter from R(alph) of Baldock, archdeacon of Middlesex, to the dean of Arches, London, certifying that he has faithfully carried out his mandate, dated at London after the Sunday on which is sung *Misericordia Domini* (the second Sunday after Easter) 128..(year invisible) to cite the abbot and convent of Westminster in the church of St Martin in the Fields to appear before the official of the court of Canterbury in Bow church on the next law day after the Sunday on which is sung the office *Jubilate* (the third Sunday after Easter) to answer the appeal in the cause between Philip, rector of Thorpe in the diocese of Norwich, and the above abbot and convent.
Dated at London, Id. April (13 April) (year invisible). Probably 1284.

WAM 20808, 22.6 × 9 cm; tongue for seal.
Endorsed: Wygod PP' Facta est coll' (late 13th cent.)
Date: Ralph of Baldock's predecessor was elected dean of St Paul's in 1276, Ralph first occurs as archdeacon of Middlesex on 25 June 1278, and was himself elected dean in October 1294 (*Fasti* i, 17). The probable date is that of other documents in the case (nos 107–117).

119. Commission from J., abbot of St Albans, delegating to the archdeacon of St Albans, the dean of Waltham Holy Cross, and the precentor of St Saviour's, Bermondsey, the papal commission to hear and determine the suit between the abbot and convent of Westminster and certain of their adversaries (unspecified).
Given at St Albans on St Bartholomew's eve (23 August) 1293.

WAM 20809, 18.6 × 9 cm; tongue for seal, and two ties. Endorsement invisible.

120. Lease from Abbot William (Colchester) and the convent of Westminster to Adam Drake, rector of Thorpe Morieux (*Murieux*) of two parts of the tithes of the fee formerly belonging to Hugh Hastynges, *miles*, called *Hastynges Fee* in the vill and fields of Thorpe Morieux and belonging to St Bartholomew's priory, to hold so long as Adam is rector thereof at a yearly rent of 13s 4d.
Given at Westminster on the morrow of Michaelmas, 1 Henry IV (30 September 1399).

WAM 20884, 29.5 × 12.8 (max.) cm; slits for seal tag; indenture, faded probably by damp. No endorsement.
Note: this is dated the day Henry IV began his reign.

121. Fragment of a grant from one Roger to St Bartholomew's of a croft and one acre and one rood of land in Thorpe (Morieux). Mid-thirteenth century.

Sciant presentes (et) futuri quod ego Rogerus de ........ et presenti (carta) mea confirmavi Ecclesie (Sancti) Bartholomei de Subiria et monachis ibidem deo servientibus croftam meam.....villa de Thorp que iacet iuxta domum Alex(andri)...ngi et unam acram terre et unam r(odam) ......apelingecroft quam predictam croftam simul et predictas acram et rodam tenuit aliquando ........ de me et heredibus meis inperpetuum liberas et quietas ab omni exaccione...... et heredibus meis annuatim pro omni servicio duodecim.........................denar' ad Pascha salva tamen ecclesie.......terre extend'.....

WAM 22859, fragment, 14.5 × 3.8 cm, now mounted on a piece of card.
Date: roughly dated by the script.

# GENERAL

122. Grant from Roger de St German to St Bartholomew's of one measure (*summa*) of wheat annually between Michaelmas and All Saints Day. Late twelfth century.

(Data per copiam.) Sciant presentes et futuri quod ego Rogerus (de Sancto Germano concessi dedi et hac carta) mea confirmaui deo et Sancto Bartholomeo de (Sudbur' et monachis ibidem deo servientibus in perpetu)am elemosinam quolibed[1] anno unam summam frumenti (reddendam inter festum Sancti Michaelis et festum) omnium Sanctorum pro salute anime mee et antecessorum meorum (uxoris mee et heredum meorum. Quare volo) et precipio quatinus predicti (monachi) ibidem deo seru(ientes prefatam elemosinam perpetue et inconcusse) a me et heredibus tenea(nt et possideant ad predictum terminum. Hiis testibus Hugone Leidet. Galfrido filio) Walteri et Thoma fratre eius. A(lano Wastinel. Waltero Hareng. Adam de Herle. Roberto de Sancto Germano. Waltero) le Bretun. Hunfrido (filio Johannis. Waltero Leidet et aliis.)

[1] B, quolibet

A. WAM 20763, fragment, late twelfth century, c. 7.8 × 10 cm. No endorsement.
B. WAM 20764, 15th century copy, 22.5 × 5.3 cm. No endorsement.
Sections of text supplied from B are given in brackets.
Date: Roger de St German witnessed *Stoke by Clare* no. 166, of 1166–80; he held land in Cavendish (*Kal Sam*, 64–5, 69). Alan Wastinel occurs in 1196–7 (Rye, *Fines*, 2).
Note: for this and similar grants see above, p. 10.

123. Copy of a confirmation by Robert son of John son of Roger de St German to St Bartholomew's of the measure of wheat given by the said Roger, to be paid in free alms yearly between Michaelmas and All Saints Day. Early thirteenth century.

Data per copiam. Sciant presentes et futuri quod ego Robertus filius Johannis Rogeri[1] de Sancto Germano ratificavi dedi et confirmavi deo et Sancto Bartholomeo iuxta Sudbur' et monachis ibidem deo servientibus illam summam frumenti quam Rogerus quondam avus meus aliquando eis dedit solvendam predictis monachis de anno in annum dictam summam frumenti inter festum Sancti Michaelis et festum Omnium Sanctorum pro salute anime mee uxoris mee heredum et antecessorum meorum. Quare volo et firmiter precipio quod predicti monachi et eorum successores hoc parvum donum meum imperpetuum habeant pro me heredibus vel assignatis meis.[1] Et ad solucionem bene et perpetualiter faciendam omnia tenementa mea obligo et maxime terras meas de Seyham et Cavenedisch' in quorumcumque manus devenerint. Hiis testibus. Johanne filio meo. Ricardo de Herle. Roberto de Sancto Germano. Hugone Breton'. Ricardo Boun. Rogero clerico et aliis.

¹ sic in ms

WAM 20765, 22.7 × 6.2 cm. 15th-century copy. No endorsement.
Date: Robert occurs in 1227–8 (*Essex Fines*, 78).


124. Grant of confraternity and participation in indulgences from Abbot
Richard and the convent of Westminster to all those who contribute to the repair
of the cell of St Bartholomew at Sudbury lately to a great extent miserably
desolated by fire and reduced to ashes and cinders, viz. a share in life and death
of all goods and spiritual benefits in the church of Westminster and its cells, and
in the churches specially joined in brotherhood with it, namely Fécamp and its
cells, Malmesbury and its cells, Malvern, Hurley, Worcester and its cells, and in
the said cell of St Bartholomew's. The abbot and convent have also obtained
from the abbot and convent of Cîteaux a share of all benefits in the Cistercian
order for benefactors to the above work. Early thirteenth century.

Vniversis sancte matris ecclesie filiis presens scriptum audituris. Ricardus dei
miseratione ecclesie Westmonasteriensis minister humilis. et eiusdem loci
conuentus, salutem in domino sempiternam. Cum per elemosinas fieri soleat
redemptio peccatorum dicente propheta, redime peccata tua elemosinis, et
mundicia elemosinam facientibus promittatur, dicente veritate in Ewangelio,
facite elemosinam, et omnia munda erunt uobis, necessaria uobis et salubris est
elemosinarum largicio, per quam premissa conferuntur. Nichil eque
peccator(um?) diligendum quam mundicia consciencie per quam anime
habitaculum emundatur. Nichil eque desiderandum penitenti ut redempcio
peccatorum qua per veniam consecuta gracia tribuitur in presenti, et in futuro
gloria eterna conferetur. Ea propter dilectissimi in reparacionem cellule Beati
Bartholomei de Sutberia nuper in magna parte per incendium miserabiliter
desolate. et in fauillam et cynerem redacte elemosinas a uobis postulantes,
precum beneficia et oracionum suffragia vobis tenemur impertiri. Nos igitur de
nostri sperantes gratia redemptoris et de meritis apostoli memorati confidentes,
cum cordis desiderio et voti sinceritate constantissima. concedimus et presentis
scripti tenore confirmamus. omnibus qui elemosinas suas ad reparationem et
reedificationem cellule memorate contulerint. uel aliud auxilium prestiterint
oportunum, participationem tam in vita quam in morte omnium bonorum et
beneficiorum spiritualium que fient in ecclesia Westmonasteriensi et cellarum
suarum in perpetuum. in missis. elemosinis. vigiliis. psalmis. et aliis bonorum
exerciciis. necnon et participationem beneficiorum que fient in ecclesiis
subscriptis que specialitate fraternitatis ecclesie nostre sunt coniuncte. Videlicet
in ecclesia Fiscannensi et cellis suis. in ecclesia Malmesberiensi et cellis suis. in
ecclesia Maluernensi. in ecclesia Herleyensi. in ecclesia Wigorniensi et cellis
suis. et in memorata cellula Sancti Bartholomei de Sutberia. Concedimus etiam
fratribus pretaxatis hoc suffragium speciale ut singulis septimanis in ecclesia
nostra pro viuis tresdecim misse celebrentur videlicet tres misse de Sancto
Spiritu. septem de Beata Virgine. et tres de Sancta Cruce. Pro defunctis eciam
fratribus qui suas elemosinas operi contulerint prelibato, viginti missas in
septimana constituimus celebrari. Ceterum de indulgencia et penitencie
relaxatione per legatos. archiepiscopos. et episcopos benefactoribus cellule

memorate suis auctenticis confirmata vos certificare dignum duximus. quorum auctoritas et potestas quingentos dies et quinquaginta de iniuncta sibi penitencia relaxauit. Preterea viginti et unus dies indulgencie auctoritate episcopali est concessa. Nos eciam a venerabili patre Abbate Cystercii participationem omnium bonorum que in ordine Cystercii fient in perpetuum benefactoribus operis prelibati impetrauimus. Ut autem tam de indulgencia prescripta quam de specialitate fraternitatis in ecclesia nostra vobis concessa ueritas innotescat, presentis scripti pagine sigilli capituli nostri duximus apponendum. Valeat uniuersitas uestra semper in domino.

> WAM 20768, 34 × 19.9 cm. Three seal tags.
> Endorsed: Fraternitas concessa omnibus benefactoribus celle beati Batholomei iuxta Sutbyr' per Ricardum Abbatem Westm' (late 13th cent.)
> Date: probably Abbot Richard de Barking, 1222–46.

125. Confirmation by John (Salmon) bishop of Norwich, in order to further religion by strengthening the religious in posession of the alms of the faithful, to St Bartholomew's of the following donations, having inspected the charters granting them: 5 acres of land in Acton (*Aketun'*) from Hamo Clerbek for the service of 1lb of pepper annually on St Bartholomew's day; half a measure (*summa*) of wheat from Bartholomew son of Ernald payable yearly on Michaelmas day at Manton (*Manetun'*); one measure of wheat from Hubert de Montchensy payable yearly on Michaelmas day at Edwardstone; one measure of wheat which the said Hubert confirmed to them of the gift of William of Goldingham payable yearly at Goldingham; half a measure of wheat from the gift of Hugh de Collingeham yearly payable from his land at Cavendish (*Cauenedis*); and of half a measure of wheat from the gift of Roger de Montchensy payable yearly at Edwardstone. Given at Braintree, 7 March 1307.

Hiis Testibus. Magistro Alexandro de Sancto Albano Willelmo capellano. Johanne de Uffingtun'. Rogero de Hamptun'. Germano clerico. Alano de Sancto Eadmundo. David de Ruddebi et aliis. Dat' apud Branketr' per manum nostram Non' Marcii pontificatus nostri anno octavo.

> WAM 20818, 17.3 × 13.1 cm. Tag for seal.
> Endorsed: Aketon' Confirmacio episcopi Norwic' de. v. acris terre in Aketon' et redditu frumenti a pluribus donatoribus collato (14th cent.)
> Date: Bartholomew son of Arnold's charter is no. 91, Hubert de Montchensy's is no. 64; Roger de Montchensy's, Hugh de Collingeham's, and Hamo Clerbek's gifts are not represented by surviving charters. See above, p. 10.

126. Copy of an inquisition *ad quod damnum* into lands held by the prior of St Bartholomew's. Early to mid-fourteenth century.
The prior and convent have 76 acres of land and 3½ acres of meadow... for the service of 2s 5d and half a pound of cumin. No relief is given from the said tenements... No heriot is given as there is no building on the tenement. As for damage (*dampnum*), they cannot judge (*nesciunt iudicare*) unless they can hold in case of escheat. They say the Lady has common rights in the tenements.

WAM 20867 dorse – see no. 48.
Date: the reference to 'the Lady' (*Domina*) is most likely to refer to Elizabeth, Lady of Clare from the death of her father Gilbert, earl of Gloucester, in 1314 to her own death in 1360. The script of the document confirms such a date.

127. Copy of an indulgence from Pope Urban V. 1362–70.
In view of the insufficient means of the priory of St Bartholomew, in which, it is said, are many relics of the saints, to support its burdens, and in order to encourage the alms of the faithful, the pope relaxes one year and forty days of enjoined penance to those truly penitent and confessed who visit and bestow alms on the church of St Bartholomew's on the festivals of Christmas, the Circumcision, Epiphany, Easter, Ascension Day, Whitsun, Corpus Christi, and the Nativity, Annunciation, Purification and Assumption of the Virgin, the Nativity of St John the Baptist, Sts Peter and Paul, St Bartholomew the Apostle, the dedication of the church, and All saints, and at the octaves of Christmas, Epiphany, Easter, Ascension, Corpus Christi, the Assumption, the Nativity of St John the Baptist and Sts Peter and Paul, and for six days after Whitsun.
Note calculating totals of indulgences: this bull, annually 95 years 140 days; from archbishops and bishops, 1,040 years; whence each day 2 years 310 days. In addition Thomas, bishop of Norwich conceded 40 days and ratified and confirmed all episcopal indulgences. Total 1,135 years 40 days per year.

WAM 20877, 28.7 × 13.1 cm, mutilated; no sign of sealing, no endorsement.

128. Another copy of 127.

WAM 20878, 26.4 × 12.2 cm; no sign of sealing, no endorsement.
Note: the purpose of 127 and 128 is not clear. They may possibly be surviving sale copies of indulgences, or publicity material of some kind. The editor is grateful for the help of Dr Robert Swanson with these documents.

129. Grant from Nicholas (de Litlyngton) abbot, and the convent of Westminster to John, warden (*custos*), and the chaplains of St Gregory's college, Sudbury, of one messuage, 210 acres of land, 1½ acres of meadow, 15 acres of pasture, rents of 23s and 1lb of pepper, 4½ quarters of wheat, one cock, one hen and one 'precare' in autumn, in the vills of Sudbury, (Long) Melford, Bulmer, Thorpe Morieux, Acton, Middleton, Cavendish, Brundon and Edwardstone, which messuage, lands and tenements are called the priory of St Bartholomew of Sudbury; in exchange for one messuage and three shops in St Michael's parish, Cornhill, London, late belonging to John Triple; warranty against all people.
Given 20 February 4 Richard II (1382)

WAM 20882, indenture, 27.9 × 16.1 (max.) cm; slits for seal tag.
No endorsement.
Note: BL Add. Ch. 47671 is the sale by John Triple, citizen and fishmonger of London, to Simon (of Sudbury), bishop of London, of a tenement in *Lombardeshall* in the parish of St Michael, Cornhill, London, dated 1371.

130. Inventory of chattels and goods pertaining to St Bartholomew's. Late fourteenth century.

First in the chapel: one gilt cross; one part of the arm of St Bartholomew; one strand (*singulum*) of the hair of St Mary; two red chasubles; three albs with one stole and maniple of no value; one portable altar (*superaltare*); two altar cloths for the altar with a frontal; one chalice with paten; one coverlet for the altar; one towel for the altar; one bottle (*uter*) of tin (*stanno*) for wine; two flasks (*ampulle*) of tin; two candlesticks of bronze (*auricalco*); one large candle (*torchyd'*); one missal; one temporal; one *Sanctorum*;[1] one portiforium; one new *Charte Warin'*;[1] one old book for burying the dead; one ordinal of no value; one very strong chest (*scista*) to put vestments in; three benches (*formule*) of six feet in length; three benches of eight feet in length; one bronze holy water stoup (*halu Waterstope*); one small bell (*tintinabulum*); another larger bell (*campana maior*); two pounds of wax for the chapel.

For the hall: one *decer* with six cushions (*cussyns*) and two bench-covers (*bankeris*); one chair (*chathedra*); three table-tops (*tabule*) with two pairs of 'chrystals' (*cristellorum*); one table-top of *mawne*[2] with two benches; one *pelmo*[3] with a ewer (*lavatorium*); one tank (*cisterna*) of tin for keeping water for the hands, with two towels; one pair of tongs (*forcipum*).

For the... Two table-cloths (*mappe*) for the prior's table; one towel; one canvas table-cloth for the table (*tabula*) of the servants; two *galunboll'*;[4] two two-quart bottles (*potelbollis*); two bronze candlesticks; one tin salt-cellar (*sallarium*); one *macatorium*;[1] one pair of pepper mills (*moli piperalis*); two casks (*cadi*) each holding (*continens*) twenty-eight gallons (*lagenas*); two other casks each holding twelve gallons; one *stonde*[1] of board (*borde*) holding six gallons; one pot (*olla*) for beer holding six gallons; three pots each holding five gallons; one *vernisbarell*;[5] one leap[6] for oatmeal (*othemele*) each holding seven feet; two large panniers (*paner'*) and two small ones; one-and-a-half gallons of honey.

In the larder (*lardario*): one large salt-trough (*saltetrow*); one-and-a-half hams (*pernia de bakunes*); five salt fish (*pisses salses*); five great bushels of salt.

In the kitchen (*quoquina*): one brazen (*enea*) pot holding three-and-a-half gallons; another pot holding two-and-a-half gallons; another pot holding six quarts (*iii potell'*); another pot holding three quarts; one metal pot (*possenet*) holding two quarts (*i potellum*); one cauldron (*cawdrun*) holding fifteen gallons; one pan (*panne*) holding five gallons; another holding one gallon; one iron spit (*spytte*) eight feet long with one hook (*grome*); iron fire-dogs (*awndyryn*); two iron bowls (*crates*); one iron tripod; six platters (*plateres*), six dishes (*dissys*), six saucers (*sawcers*) of pewter (*pute*); four platters of wood with twenty dishes and seven saucers; one dressing-knife (*dressynknyf*) with two knives (*cultellis*) for the kitchen; one *weston'*;[7] one dressing-stock (*dressynstoke*); one cowl (*covel*)[8] for keeping water in the kitchen; one pail (*payle*); half a pipe (*pipe*) for keeping *wasche*;[1] two iron pothooks (*pottehokys*); one mortar (*mortyr*); one large axe (*securis*); one bill (*byll*); one flesh-hook (*fleschehoke*); one bowl (*bolle*); one *cheryn*[9] with three...

In the bakehouse (*pistrina*): one large oven (*fornax*) holding fifty-four gallons; another small one holding twenty gallons; one mashing-vat (*maschefat*) holding six bushels and another holding three bushels; one steeping-vat (*stepynkfatte*) holding twelve bushels; one *zelingfate*;[1] three keelers (*kelers*);[10] three tubs (*tubb'*) each holding eight gallons; one cowl (*covyll*) holding sixteen gallons; one *uletubbe;*[1] two kneading-troughs (*knedyngtrowys*) and three other small ones; one grinding-quern (*gryndynquerne*); one cleansing-sieve (*clensygseue*) for beer; two *cyffeyns;*[11] half a *yinhayre;*[1] three mats (*matthys*) for malt.[12]

In the chamber: one good press (*presse*) to put cloths (*vestibus*) in; one excellent chest (*cista optima*) to put various things in; ... one ...*nysthorne*...

In the barn (*orreo*): one plough bound with iron; another plough without iron (*non ferrata*); one tumbril (*tumberell'*); two long ladders and two small ones; one fan (*fanne*) in the barn; three pitchforks (*pyccheforke*); wheat, three quarters; William Rowode owes one-and-a-half quarters of wheat; two bushels of wheat in the granary (*garnario*); four bushels of mixtil (mixed corn) (*mestyloy*); total, three quarters and (six) bushels; oats, by estimate five quarters; *haras,*[13] two quarters; peas, seven quarters; total, fourteen quarters; for the ploughs (*aratris*), beams (*bemys*), *haulys,*[1] share-beams (*reys*), straddles (*stradelis*), *grondys*[1] enough (*sufficienter*) for one year; two *cuherys*[1] with two ploughshares; one harrow (*herpica*); one seed basket (*sedelepe*); one *spryngynskepe;*[1] everything for the ploughs, two cart saddles (*cartesadel'*), traces (*trayse*), collars (*coler*) for six horses; one good cart-rope (*cartherope*); five halters (*capistra*) made of leather; three *parea wyll*[1] with three locks (*seris*); three dung-forks (*dungforkys*) with two flanges (*fallangis*).

Livestock: ...six horses, two oxen, two cows, one boar, one sow, six pigs for the larder with six piglets; six geese with two ganders; forty-six capons and hens with chicks; ten hives for bees (*apiaria pro apibus*); two sheep; in the barn remain by estimate ten quarters of barley in sheaves; in the granary remain five quarters of barley malt; twelve acres sown well and seasonably (*sesinabiliter*) with wheat and in the field forty-four acres stand well for sowing barley, and for peas, *haras*, and oats thirty acres; of hay there remains hay of seven acres and of *palsa*[1] enough for all the year and of strewing-straw (*stramine*) enough for all the year; one *bresyldehors,*[1] 5s; three horses (*equi*), three marks; two oxen, 40s; one horse, 20d; cart harness (*cartheharnays*) 12d; one shod cart (*schodecarte*), two marks; two cows, 20s; (erasure)

| | |
|---|---|
| 1 unidentified | 8 a large portable tub |
| 2 probably timber | 9 churn? |
| 3 or 'pelino' – unidentified | 10 wide shallow tub for cooling liquids |
| 4 gallon bottles? | 11 cups? |
| 5 varnished barrel? | 12 to lay malt on when drying |
| 6 a dry measure | 13 a kind of pulse grown for animal feed |
| 7 whetstone? | |

WAM 20880, 25 × 24 cm.
Endorsed: (14th cent.) Inventar' celle de Sudbery
Date: the script; possibly associated with no. 129.

131. Appointment by George (Fascet), abbot of Westminster, of Dom Thomas Flete, fellow monk of Westminster, to be prior of St Bartholomew's for the term of his life, to grant him some rest after his strenuous labours; provided that he shall obey the abbot's mandates, and maintain and repair the place.
Given in the Chapter House at Westminster, 29 July 1499.

WAM 20887, 27.6 × 14.2 cm. No endorsement.
Two seals on tags: left, Abbot Fascet's seal: red wax, fragment, 2.9 × 3.5 cm: Our
Lord between St George and St Edward.
Right: convent seal: dark brown wax, fragment, 6.5 × 5.0 cm; central figures only –
very clear impression.

# INDEX

Numbers in italic refer to pages in the Introduction; those in roman type to the charters by number.

# Previously published volumes of Suffolk Charters

XIII EYE PRIORY CARTULARY AND CHARTERS
PART TWO
*ed. V. Brown*

XIV CHARTERS OF THE MEDIEVAL HOSPITALS
OF BURY ST EDMUNDS
*ed. C. Harper-Bill*